FOOD OUT OF CHILE

RECIPES AND STORIES
FROM MARIA FIGUEROA

I dedicate this book to British solidarity and specifically to the North East of England who supported me and the Chilean people. My life in exile has been bearable thanks to the understanding and confidence of friends, solidarity groups for Latin America and mainly the encouragement and determination of the Red Herring Workers' Co-op and the remarkable support and encouragement of my family in every task and aim I undertook.

Maria Figueroa
Newcastle uponTyne
August 1990

British Library Cataloguing in Publication Data
Figueroa Zuñiga, Maria *1938-*
    Food out of Chile : recipes and stories from Maria Figueroa.
    1. Vegetarians. Food. Chilean dishes. Recipes
    I. Title   II. Red Herring Workers' Co-operative
    641.5360983

    ISBN 0-907367-07-0
    ISBN 0-951662-20-1

© Maria Figueroa 1990

Co-published by

Earthright Publications
8 Ivy Avenue
Ryton, Tyne and Wear
NE40 3PU

ISBN 0 907367 07 0

and

Red Herring Workers' Co-operative
4 Studley Terrace
Fenham
Newcastle upon Tyne
NE4 5AH

ISBN 0 9516622 0 1

Typeset and printed at Tyneside Free Press Ltd
5 Charlotte Square
Newcastle upon Tyne
NE1 4XF
on recycled paper

Earthright Publications ISBN 0 907467 07 0
Red Herring Workers' Co-operative ISBN 0 9516622 0 1

CONTENTS

Photographs

INTRODUCTION

Maria Figueroa had to flee the dreadful persecution following the fascist coup d'état in Chile in 1973 when the democratically elected government of Salvador Allende was overthrown by General Pinochet with massive U.S.A. assistance. In the months following, over 70,000 people were tortured, murdered or "disappeared". Eventually Maria and her family came to Newcastle, and with the experience of years of cooking for the family it was another step to make food in large quantities to sell to others. It is not an easy thing to do but it is an extension of a domestic skill. Maria and her family realised the possibilities of introducing Latin American food to people in the region at various events and eventually with the Red Herring Workers' Co-op.

Over the years they have raised a lot of money this way for causes in Latin America and elsewhere; it is not an easy way to make money! It is an ancient tradition though, so many poor people throughout time and throughout the world sell food they have made to survive. Likewise, Maria's aspilleras, her political patchworks, are an extension of another domestic skill which becomes an act of resistance practised by political prisoners, families of the disappeared, the repressed and exiled. They express experiences and hopes to be displayed and also sold to make a little money; sometimes this is the only source of income. Her experiences and choices are a reflection of so many women in adversity, developing what skills they have for their survival and that of their family and their dignity.

The title *Food Out Of Chile* has the meaning of food and survival in exile, but also implies recipes from other Latin American countries which Maria has collected from her friends over the years.

Maria has wanted to make a book of her recipes for a long time. The return of Maria Figueroa and her compañero, Victor Fenick, to Chile in autumn 1990 has inspired all the compañeros and compañeras at the Red Herring Workers' Co-op to make it happen. More than just a book of recipes we also wanted to capture some of their story, their life in Chile prior to the coup, their exile and subsequent experiences. We can only hope to capture some of the flavour here but I hope you enjoy the 'mélange'!

I first met Victor, Maria and their family in 1979 when I attended various events where they would inevitably be providing food, whatever else their involvement may have been. Some time after this I had my first experience of providing food by opening the original Red Herring, a clandestine café in the west end of Newcastle.

The present Red Herring opened on February 28th 1987. I was always needing help to do the baking and run the café. I would sometimes be asked by Victor to do pizzas for the events they were organising at St Thomas' Church in town and Victor said if I needed help just call him. I wasn't really sure how keen he was but I asked him a number of times.

In early 1988 it was suggested we form a full blown workers' co-op, and we asked Victor and Maria to join us. I was really pleased they agreed but I didn't know then how significant they would be to its success.

Victor and Maria's role in the Co-op has been a very important one; their commitment and capacity for work and hardship have been an example to us all. There have been so many difficulties to overcome and often the work has been very long and hard. Victor and Maria's attitude of optimism and determination along with their maturity have given real backbone to the Co-op. Now in August 1990 we are a co-op of nine full-time workers, and in anticipating their imminent departure we will of course miss them terribly. We are all part of the family by now, and we only hope for a bright future for them and for Chile after so much loss and suffering. We will be hoping to visit them when they are established in their new home. We are forever with them in solidarity, and will, of course, support them at any time, and hope the links between us will strengthen. We are glad our work together has helped them to be able to return with optimism in spite of all difficulties. Their legacy will remain and we hope the flavour of Latin America will remain with the Co-op and with us all. The tradition of Latin American days at the Red Herring will be continued by the Nicaraguan Solidarity Campaign which Maria and Victor set up in Newcastle in 1978.

Even after years of knowing Victor and Maria it is only recently I have started to understand any of the true horrors of the fascist and bloody coup d'état in 1973. It is important for us to understand how these things come about, how they affect ordinary lives and how ordinary people organise, respond, resist; how hope manifests itself. Their life in this country has not been easy. Support for them, perhaps for all exiles, has been less than it might have been. They have maintained an impressive dignity throughout.

They have not failed to win many friends who love and admire them. I will miss them as much as anyone, but their return is not a loss to me but a great triumph and inspiration which gives me strength and humility. It is a pleasure to know and to work with them and to be thought of as their compañero. We wish them the very best in all their work and lives 'back home', with the setting up of community projects, for a new Chile and a New World free from fascism and violence.

Nigel Wild

Red Herring Workers' Co-operative
August 1990

Acknowledgements

Photographs by Charles Biggs and Alice King
Cover design and illustrations by Meg McDermott
Introduction by Nigel Wild
Glossary by Jane Becconsall
Special thanks to: Victor Fenick, Raquel Fenick Figueroa, Fiona Bates, Matthew Davison, Andy Smith, Gwen Terry, Chris Ford, Ken Grant, Mark Jan, and Carol Stephenson; and Monica Frisch for helping to make it all happen. General support, encouragement and good food from everyone at the Red Herring café;
and all the people who taught Maria recipes.

Weights and Measures

Abbreviations		**Exact conversions**	
g	= gramme	1000 grammes	= 1 kilogram
kg	= kilogram	1 kilogram	= 2.204 pounds
lb	= pound	1 pound	= 454 grammes
oz	= ounce	1 ounce	= 28.35 grammes
		100 grammes	= 3.527 ounces
fl oz	= fluid ounce	20 fluid ounces	= 1 pint
l	= litre	1 litre	= 1.76 pints
ml	= millilitre	1000 millilitres	= 1 litre
		1 pint	= 568 millilitres
tsp	= teaspoon	1 tsp (level)	= 5ml
tbsp	= tablespoon	1 tbsp (level)	= 3 tsp = 15 ml
cm	= centimetre	1 centimetre	= 0.394 inches
"	= inch	1 inch	= 2.54 centimetres

Notes on ingredients are given in the glossary.

If you want to know what things taste like, go to the Red Herring Café which serves many of them! Most of the beans and dried ingredients can be bought from the Red Herring shop.

This is based on conversations between Maria Figueroa, Victor Fenick, her husband and compañero, and other members of the Red Herring Workers' Co-operative, in August 1990.

Why leave Chile?

Victor and Maria, I would like to ask you why it is that you have found yourselves in England? Why did you leave Chile?

M   The reasons are political reasons. We noticed that the circles were getting narrower and narrower, and through the advice of some friends, especially some nuns with whom we used to work together in the community, we took the decision to leave, because we were very much afraid for our family.

And this was in 1973?

M   Yes, that was 1973.

So what lead to that situation? What was happening? What was it about your involvement which made it impossible for you to stay?

V   Well, probably people know that in October 1970 for the first time in Latin America was a president elected who lead a left wing coalition. This government started to make radical changes in the country, not just politically but economically. There was a possibility to build a new society with this new government but, because we did not have all the power in our hands, we only had the presidential power, we did not have the power of the senate or of the armed forces or of the media, little by little right wing elements began to take control of everything. They did not want us to be successful because it would be a very bad example for other Latin American countries who were suffering the same as we were suffering before 1970. And then they bought a coup d'état. The first attempt was on 29th June 1970 and it failed because some of the armed forces were loyal to the government, but on 11th September 1973 they managed to make a coup d'état. As soon as the coup d'état came, the repression started and the oppression was so fierce, we had never seen before in our country the way this repression was. They killed the political leaders of the left wing parties, the trade unionists, people in the health service, teachers, musicians, leaders of the communities, and so on and so on; women, men, old men, old women, everyone they considered dangerous for the state. And because we were both leaders in our community and because some of our friends warned us, some of our friends the nuns came to see us and said it was quite dangerous for us to stay. In the beginning we did not want to leave the country, we wanted to stay, but little by little the circle became narrower and narrower and then we took the final decision to leave the country. I left first to Lima, Peru, disguised as a tourist. I left behind Maria and the children and they followed in March 1974. I left on 29th December 1973.

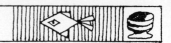

So the danger arose primarily because of your activity in the community rather than your trade union activity?

V Yes, because Maria was a leader in the community, helping our new government. The government tried to create a body which would take care of the distribution of food because the black marketeers started to appear in Chile, the owners of the food stores began to hide the food to create the illusion that the government was so bad there was no food. Maria was vice president of this organisation, the Junta de Abastecimientos y Control de Precios (J.A.P.) to fight against this, and in that way she gained the hate of these other people. For my part I was elected as president of the parents' association of one of the big schools in the area with 2,500 children. My job was to work to try to improve the situation at the school, to try to make the life of the children more happy, but they were so short of things but we tried to do it. Also I was involved in political campaigns in support of the government.

When did you first get involved in political activity, Victor?

V I was really very involved in 1970 after the election of the Allende government. Before that I was fighting alone quite a lot of the time without any organisation except for the trade union to which I belonged.

So have you always been in the trade union?

V Well, we created the union with other bus drivers in about 1963 because we realised it was the only way to defend our rights against the bosses, and then I became well marked by the bosses; they used to call me red, sometimes as a joke, but a lot of the time very seriously.

But you still managed to keep a job, Victor?

V Yes, this was one of the contradictions in life. They thought I was a good worker – I was a very reliable worker – they let me keep the job because they knew I was reliable and looked after the buses. I was always clean not dirty, according to them I was very honest. I knew I was an honest man, this was nothing new to me! I was never driving drunk or dirty, in that way they respected me.

How active was your union, Victor, from 1963?

V We were really active, we gained quite a lot of things. For example we gained respect when we held a successful strike about pay, they did not believe that we could, and we won! That was in 1965 or '66. The strike was only in the bus company I worked for but we did get support from others, and we paralysed the city because other people joined us and it was Christmas and New Year when there is a big demand for public transport; in a way we created chaos but we won the strike. After that they gave us uniforms for work, before that we had to wear our own clothes.

What was happening towards the end of this time, before the Allende government? Was there a general feeling among ordinary people that things could be done, that it was possible to elect a socialist government?

V   The political and democratic situation at that time in the '70s was that the right wing coalition had not any possibility in the view of the working class, and people began to see the possibility of seeing a change in society. For example the health situation was really bad, the hospital was always short of doctors or beds. We have a good example of that. I don't remember which one of our sons it was, but when one of them was born I went to the hospital to see Maria in the maternity ward and I found Maria in the same bed with another woman, two women in the same bed with their babies! I couldn't believe it could be possible, there could have been an infection or something. But that was very normal in Chile and people used to die in hospital waiting to be seen to. In the schools all there was was a teacher and a blackboard, there was never enough, sometimes there was not even a piece of chalk to write on the board. The law said that primary education in Chile was free and mandatory but what is the point of going to school if you have no teacher? The workers most of the time were persecuted by the bosses when they went on strike, and they used force, they used the police, sometimes they used the army, to finish the working class; in general it was a situation that was very bad for the working class Chilean people. For example we have a very big textile industry in Chile but most of the factories were working about 50% or 60% of their capacity. When Allende took power, one of the first things he did, apart from giving half a litre milk free to every child to the age of eight or nine, then he started to put the factories to work full.

And this increased employment?

V   Absolutely; from a factory working 60% capacity to 100% production it put more people in jobs. One of the big unions, the building workers, joined the carpenters and the metal workers, and Allende put them to work building houses for the poor people. Things began to change, they put more people in the hospital, they passed a law to be mandatory that a person in hospital had to be attended, and many people might think that it was quite easy to do that, but the other way they did not do it.

M   Another thing was the national prescription where you could buy drugs very cheaply, medicines. The doctor or hospital could prescribe you medicines, the prices were very very cheap, everyone could afford to buy them. That was one of their great achievements.

It seems that a lot of the changes that Allende made were revolutionary but he came to power democratically.

V   Well it was a revolution in a sense because never never before had it happened that a socialist government or a socialist coalition had formed a government. In January 1971 there was a council election and the left wing coalition won around 53% of the vote; in the presidential election we had won 38% so it was a big increase. In March 1973 for the senate, for the MPs,

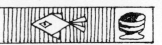

for the lower house, despite all the problems we have at that time, we had 43% of the electorate with us, and this was never seen before. This was one of the main reasons they made the coup because they knew that in 1976 in the next general election we would win.

M   It was great to see! You could hear working class people on the bus saying 'I've got money to buy shoes for my children, I am going to take them to the beach'; they were thinking what to do, just thinking for the future, that was one very important thing; thinking in the future because we knew what we could achieve. For the first time they could go to the hospital and they were free and if the doctor give you a prescription it was free and the medicines were cheap, you could afford it, it wasn't a problem. And at school the children had a meal and they had books and teachers; it was really something, just everything appeared, it was amazing, it was really amazing. It was a revolution really for everybody involved, for the community really, it was so important because people began to reorganise again and to improve their knowledge, that was very important.

So in a way the Allende government precipitated a lot of community activity. It was not necessarily that Allende was elected because of the community activity but he made the possibilities?

M   Yes, because when people saw the first decree that Allende made in the campaign was to nationalise our national wealth, the first law was to expropriate the copper mines, and he did not matter how much pressure was put on him by the U.S.A. who owned the companies, he did it and people never believed he could do it! Some people, even including some of us, could not believe that he would be able to do it, but when he did it was a day of pride for Chilean people. And that way people began to feel that everything was possible and things began to rise from the bottom! And another thing that was important was that for the first time people were thinking to send their children to the university because you could get a grant, so the children could go and study and have a different chance than their parents.

What would you say about Allende the man? What was he like?

M   He was a great man, he really was special. He never deceived us, he always told us the problems, the reality, and we followed him, he was a very conscious man. But he made a mistake, to trust the bourgeoisie, that was a mistake.

You said there were men in the military that were allies?

M   Well quite a lot of military officers were supportive of the new processes, not especially of Allende but of the new changes in the country, because they also began to realise that there was the possibility of creating change. That was quite good and we have mention General Bachelet who was in charge of the distribution of food. He had the power to do that because he was a general and he could mobilise lorries for food distribution. A lot of officers

were like this. I remember that the school of the young officers who were loyal to Allende, the day of the coup, they were inside the building at a meeting and they were all killed.

How many were there?

M About twenty five. It is important to mention the new generation of officers were just loyal to Allende for the period when he was elected.

You said that Allende's mistake was to trust the bourgeoisie.

M Yes, because to trust the bourgeoisie is to maintain the legal system, and of course the majority of the bourgeoisie were Christian democratic and the nationalist party.

You said that then the conditions began to improve for ordinary people, were the conditions of the bourgeoisie worsening or were they doing quite well too?

V They were doing quite well because one of the things that we disagreed with the government about was the expropriation, the expropriation of a factory for example, they paid back to the owners for what was taken and this gave the owners more power to create black markets. I didn't agree with that but Allende said to us, 'listen, I promised to work within our constitution and I have to do that because I have to act according to the constitution', and we say, 'why not change the constitution?'. Probably he wanted that but probably it was not the time to do it and they had to secure what they had; this is one of the discussions that we still have in Chile, the things we did not agree with the government on.

During all of this time how aware were you of the activities of the U.S.A. in supporting the government prior to Allende and then supporting the right wing elements during the Allende government?

V Since the very beginning. In October 1970 the commander in chief of the army, General Schneider, was shot dead in an ambush by the right wing. He supported the constitution and he said he would obey the law and support the government because it was freely elected by the people. It was in the constitution that the army should support the wish of the people and that was quite something. Allende was elected September 4th and on November 4th took charge of the country. This assassination was planned to stop Allende taking power, but the plot failed because the man who succeeded him, General Pratt, was also a constitutionalist. But on the day of the coup he was under house arrest. And then the military freed him and he went to Buenos Aires, and then they sent one of Pinochet's men to kill him and they put a bomb under his car and killed him and his wife.

So were you always aware that the U.S.A. was supporting the right wing elements?

M Well we were aware, but unfortunately the media was in right wing hands, we had only one station, the Catholic station, and it was very dubious, they were in the middle playing both sides, we knew that.

Maria, can you tell us more about your involvement in the community organisation?

M The first organisation I joined was the Mothers' Association in 1963, and later I joined the Junta de Vecinos, the neighbourhood association, in '65.
And did you live in the Conchali area since you were married?

M No, we moved in 1960 from some other area of the city to that area, from '60 to '73 we lived in that area.
What was the area like, was it very poor?

M Working class, yes, a working class area and surrounded by shanty towns. But we had a proper house.

V A rented house.
Did you feel that you were poor?

M We felt we were very poor, we just managed with Victor working overtime just to feed the children, all the time 14, 16 hours a day.

V I was one of the lucky who could do that.
What would happen if somebody was ill and couldn't work? Was there any benefits system?

V Not at all. During the Allende government if you worked for a private boss you have to reach some sort of agreement that they will pay you some benefit, but it was really difficult. There were so many things during the three years we wanted to do but we couldn't, there were other priorities. But with the trade union we managed to make some agreement with the bosses sometime. But going back, when Maria joined this community centre, the Mothers' Association, it wasn't really political, it was more a workshop and community centre,

M sharing skills and helping each other.

V It was a mothers' group. But later after the election, I was one day thinking alone, I say, 'Victor, you always talk about changes, but you did not join any organisation and you cannot still sit around', and I decided, I went to the address of one of the branch of the socialist party, I asked them, I want to join. When I did that I told Maria, 'Maria, I did this thing, I'm not sure whether it's safe, I will be very pleased if you want to join with me in this but it is up to you, it's for you to decide, I will be very happy if you join me'. Maria didn't answer me at this very moment, but later she said she would and she joined the same branch, and a couple of months and she was called to be in charge of the Junta de Abastecimientos y Control de Precios (food distribution and price control organisation) as a vice president.
So was the socialist party very active in the Barrios? ('Barrios' means district but is only used of poor areas.)

V Yes, we had a very good branch.

M The one who always caught my attention was Allende's sister, she was really a good activist, she went to the community to any meeting and chat with the people.

V   She visit the campamentos, the shanty town that just appear without any shelter, just blanket and sheet (like a tent) and a Chilean flag. The authorities have to respect the Chilean flag so they feel more secure if their home includes one. This was an old law. They were all over the country, and they start to make, built the shanty town, and she used to go there to talk to the people, support the people, fighting in the parliament. The socialist party in the area had a lot of very honest people. I was quite happy when I was working with them in Chile in my barrio.

So were they people living locally like yourselves who had just joined or were there a lot of people who had been in the socialist party for many years?

V   Both. The number of people who joined the socialist party after the election was quite high. I was one of the new ones to join then; the party grows in number quite dramatically, probably not in quality but in quantity. I attend the first meeting, my political education start from reading the papers and then someone gave me some books and little by little I was gaining in confidence in myself.

Maria, tell us a bit about your involvement in the community, the neighbourhood association and your election as vice president of the Junta de Abastecimientos y Control de Precios.

M   It was difficult at that moment, especially because there were a lot of Christian democratic party members in the Junta de Vecinos and they tried to create the atmosphere, everything was struggle and was wrong from the Allende government. Instead to be more understanding and to help the neighbourhood, they create division. I remember we struggled just to maintain our level of commitment which was really increasing and the involvement of the community was very high at that moment. It was a lot of good ideas, a lot of good points which we tried to pass through the Association for the improvement of the community, especially to improve the conditions in the shanty towns where people had no electricity, no water, no proper sanitation, which was the first priority. We had a lot of problems to get through the local council to approve that. It really was hard to cope with all the problems for the people and confusing what steps should be taken to maintain united government policy of Allende in our council. From then we started taking a kind of popular power through the control of the distribution of food in the local areas, through the Junta de Abastecimientos y Control de Precios (J.A.P.).

How did you do that? This was to overcome the profiteering of black marketeers, the shop owners who were stockpiling goods?

M It was quite hard. Luckily I had the support of our political party in our area and also the support of my companero, Victor, and my children, because the children had to cook, the children had to wash, to look after Raquel, she was a baby. In 1970/71 Rodrigo was 12 and Eduardo was 13, and they were involved in their school, in the youth student organisation.

This was the school you were involved with?

M Exactly. The children, the two oldest ones, they make a lot of voluntary work at the weekends, especially they went to the railway station to lift, to unload the lorries.

To help with the food distribution?

M Yes, to help with carrying food, they were quite energetic, they were inspired I think by the whole atmosphere in the school, it was something to do. We make things to improve those conditions, at the same time we were demanding of our government to give more chances, to give more power to us, to J.A.P.

Did you feel they were willing to do that?

M At some stage, yes. For example, Albert Bachelet who was very much aware of how important was the popular power and to stop the black market in food by getting centralised distribution. I think he was the mastermind to increase popular power for that reason. After the coup he was killed.

Did you meet him?

M Yes I have met him.

V He was a general from the airforce.

He was assassinated?

V Yes, in jail. One morning the guards went to his cell and found him hung, but he was so weak, he was ill, he could not hang himself. It wasn't possible for him to take his own life, he was killed.

So how did you try and organise the food distribution, Maria? What was the process?

M Well the first thing we did we went door to door asking people to give their support, if they allow us to take their name and the number of people who were living there who prefer the solution of the J.A.P. scheme. Well some people, very few, just close their door in our faces and they call us communists or whatever, but we kept doing that for quite a while until we were really quite well organised at least for our area and we started to organise the distribution with the support of local people. The control was made by us, that was the main thing, we knew when the food is going to arrive, and we receive the food, and when the owner of the shop tried to deceive the people we struggled against this; we said, 'no, that's the law, the government, we have to respect it'. Many times we were threatened by people, shop owners and some of them worse than threaten, tried to buy us offering, 'would you like a sack of rice? would you like a sack of sugar? we

can get something for you because you work too much and you don't have time', but we always said 'no' because we are in the list exactly like everybody else.

Were you also involved in this, Victor?

V Yes, helping Maria in this thing because I was so afraid of someone coming to do something to Maria. In that way I think it was a macho thing; helping Maria to do something when I knew she could do it without me.

M I had a lot of support also from a lot of youth from our area. They decided, every day, all the time when I am going to distribute the food to have two of them behind me and they made rotas. I felt supported, I gained so much confidence from them, just teenagers, committed because they knew they can do something.

V They say to me sometime, 'don't be worried, we'll take care of her, no-one will touch her'.

And did they have any trouble?

M Mario, only Mario, he was threatened many times, because he was a hair dresser; we don't know what happened to him.

V He had to hide, we lose contact with him and the young people of our branch after the coup, because people started to be terrified, afraid. We cannot afford to have meeting because there were quite a lot of informers in there as well. It was quite dangerous, it was forbidden, any meeting was forbidden, we cannot have a meeting, there cannot be more than two people in the same place at one time. That's why people do a trick, they have some meeting in the house or bar watching the football match and they talk about political things and having the meeting in there, and they look like a football watcher, it's a lot of trick. Or they go to the cemetery, they say, 'we are going to see a relative who has just died' and they went to stand in front of the grave and they were talking politics.

This was after the coup?

V Yes, 3 or 4 months and after that.

Did you have to meet like that, meet your friends and comrades in that way?

V No, I meet them in the street sometimes, but what really happened was in October, when we start to think to leave the country. I went to the branch of the socialist party. I knew one of the leader was still living in there, I went for advice from him. I knocked on the door and after a while the doors open and he was there. He wasn't the same companero as I knew before, it was an absolute shame, I think he was really terrified. I said 'I want to talk to you if possible', and he said 'yes, right but very quickly'. I said, 'the situation is that we are under pressure, we are under threat and we are afraid to be called by the police, and we don't want to be called by the police because what will happen to our children? But I want to ask your advice, shall I leave the country? Shall I stay? What the party say?'. And he said, 'do what you please'. I said, 'that's all?'. He said, 'I'm sorry, there is no party any longer' and he said to me, 'don't bother me again'.

Were you very disheartened by that, Victor? Did you think there should be more grit?

V   Oh yes, I was absolutely disillusioned because for the three years I was in the party I fought very hard to create it as an organisation and I supposed that everyone like me would do the same. If the party say that every member shall stay in the country, I will, no matter what happen to my family I will stay, the party is one. But now there is no party and I went back to talk to Maria and I explain the situation, I say to Maria, 'I don't want to make a decision now, we have to wait until November now, I think there is no way'.

Were you still working as a bus driver at that time, Victor?

V   I was a casual worker. I was working with Catholic priests' school since 1967, I was working with them as a private driver for the school, but I work part time in the company as well to make some more money for the family. The year I put the children in that school, I change them from the primary school they were at, and the party talked to me and said, 'Victor, we need you as president of the parents' association. It's a political decision, you have to go'. At the school we had a big hall and all the parents came in and they proclaim candidates. First we answer questions and then people start to vote and I won by a majority of probably 99%. I was very surprised and people who didn't know me very well or knew me only as a bus driver vote for me. And we start to develop a plan to refurbish the school with minimum resources, painting, repairing the toilets because they were in a bloody mess, the toilets for the children, and asking the shop owners to give free something, some knobs or fittings or something, some paintbrush, roller. We had to collect them and we had to do voluntary jobs, convince the other parents to come one Sunday to do the painting and the plastering and little by little we were doing things.

So it was really hard work, Victor?

V   The most hard was to find the time. I had to go to meetings, do quite a lot of the voluntary jobs on the Sunday when I need to have a rest because I work in the minibuses and go to party meetings, help Maria in the distribution of foods. We do not have the time to think sometime, just to know there are things that have to be done and you have to do them.

M   Sometime we did not see each other and my mother she did not understand.

V   She ask me, 'why are you doing things for other people and you don't take care of your own son?' I said, 'I am taking care of my son, but I have more sons outside and I have more brothers than my brothers, the people are my brother and my son, I have to take care of them as well' and she couldn't understand that.

M   We make mistakes as well, just to be so respectful of the bourgeois law which was never on our side, always was on the opposition. But we learnt a good lesson and a few things which I really regret sometime and I think we have been quite upset by homesickness, but the main thing have been we never deceived our people, we have been always working for them.

Concentrado para Sopa
Vegetable stock

Chile
Vegan

If you are strictly vegetarian do not throw away any green leaves or stalks or left overs from freshly made salads.

Left over green leaves and stalks from salads
2 or 3 potatoes
1 head of garlic
Pieces of onion, carrots, celery and peppers
Tied bunch of parsley

Cover the ingredients with cold water and boil for 15 minutes. Strain and keep the liquid as stock.

Selection of vegetables as above
2 tbsp oil or margarine
2 bay leaves
pinch cumin
dash oregano
dash paprika

Fry the vegetables in hot oil, stirring constantly. Add bay leaves and spices and a little water and boil for 15 minutes. Cool and liquidize and use as a concentrated stock.

Sopa de Avena Arrollada
Soup made with rolled oats

Venezuela
serves 4

60–80 g (2–3 oz) oats
1½ l (2½ pints) stock, homemade or from stock cubes
2 tbsp margarine
3 tbsp cream
2 tbsp parsley, chopped

Fry the oats in the margarine very quickly, then cook them in the stock for 10 minutes over a low flame. Add more liquid as necessary.

Just before serving add cream and parsley.

Victor's Vegetable Soup

serves 8
Vegan

I have made this for the Red Herring. It is a big, filling, nourishing soup. With bread you could make a good meal.

1 medium swede, diced
2 large onions, coarsely chopped
300 g (11 oz) carrots, sliced
1 green pepper, seeded and sliced
1 red pepper, seeded and sliced
1 small cauliflower, cut into florets
½ savoy cabbage
oil for frying
½ tsp ground cumin
½ tsp oregano
½ tsp dried parsley
½ tsp sweet paprika
pinch mint
pinch cayenne
salt and pepper

Fry all the vegetables in hot oil, adding spices when they start to brown. Add 3 l (5 pints) of water and cook until the vegetables are tender. Liquidize.

Serve hot with bread.

Crema de Lechuga
Lettuce soup

Chile
serves 4

This is a summer recipe. It can be served cold.

2 lettuces and lettuce to garnish
1¼ l (2 pints) vegetable stock
1 tbsp butter
2 tbsp flour
1 tbsp cream
dash of nutmeg
salt and pepper

Clean the two lettuces very carefully and cut them finely. Put them for 2 minutes in a bowl with boiling water – this process cleans the lettuce properly. Strain and discard water.

Put the stock in a pan and cook for 10 minutes together with the lettuces, nutmeg, salt and pepper. Separately melt the butter and pour in the flour making a roux. Heat this well until you get a slight golden colour; then pour the stock in, avoid lumps, boil for 2 minutes only. Liquidize the mixture, then add a whirl of cream at the last minute before serving.

Serve in a bowl with cubes of fried bread and very thinly shredded fresh lettuce. This can be served hot or cold.

Sopa Criolla
Quick Chilean soup

Chile
serves 6
Vegan (if eggs omitted)

'Criolla' means something traditional to a country, (in this case Chile), but it is also linked to the word 'creole' which may indicate where this soup originated.

225 g (8 oz) fresh or tinned peeled tomatoes
100 g (4 oz) rice
2 onions, finely chopped
4 tbsp red sauce
3 cloves garlic, chopped very fine
2 l (3½ pints) stock or water
2 eggs (optional)
2 tbsp oil
2 tbsp parsley
pinch rosemary
salt and pepper

Fry the onions and peppers in oil for a few minutes. Add roughly chopped tomatoes, red sauce, garlic, herbs and salt and pepper, and cook a minute more. Add stock or water and bring to the boil, add rice and cook till done.

Near the end of the cooking I often add some lightly beaten egg whites; this forms white threads in the soup.

Frijoles Licuados
Creamy black bean soup

Guatemala
serves 6
Vegan

400 g (1 lb) black beans, soaked overnight
2 onions, coarsely chopped
2 cloves garlic, whole
4 tbsp oil
salt and pepper
Plain yogurt, sour cream, salty white cheese or rice to garnish
Tortillas or totopos

Rinse the beans several times and put to cook with cold water and onions, garlic and oil. Halfway through, after 35 to 40 minutes, add the salt. Liquidize and add water until the consistency is of unwhipped cream. Reheat.

Serve with plain yogurt, sour cream, salty white cheese or boiled rice sprinkled on, and tortillas or totopos.

Sopa de Porotos
Pinto bean soup

Chile
serves 8 to 10
Vegan

500 g (18 oz) pinto beans (or canneloni or flagelots)
225 g (8 oz) potatoes, diced
3 to 4 onins, finely sliced
1 green pepper, finely chopped
2 medium carrots, finely grated
3 cloves garlic, crushed
100 g (4 oz) vermicelli
generous handful spinach, very finely chopped (optional)
bread, stale for frying
3 tbsp sunflower oil
extra oil for frying
2 tsp cumin seeds
2 tsp paprika
salt

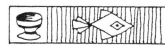

Soak the beans overnight or at least 3 hours before you plan to cook. Boil them in 4 l (7 pints) water with the cumin seeds; half way through add 2 tsp salt. Keep stock with beans.

Fry onions, peppers, grated carrots and garlic. Add paprika, parsley and salt and mix with the cooked beans and their cooking liquid. Bring to the boil and add the potatoes and spinach (if you have). Cook for 3 to 4 minutes, then crush vermicelli in your hand and pour in. Boil for a further 3 minutes.

Fry slices and square pieces of stale bread and put on top when you serve, plus a dash of paprika.

Sopa de Espinacas   *Chile*
Spinach soup   serves 4 to 6
                                   Vegan (if garnish omitted)

This dish is basic for children; it's so good for them.

1½ l (2½ pints) vegetable stock
650 g (1½ lb) fresh spinach, cut off the stalks
300–350 g (11 or 12 oz) potatoes, diced
6 medium onions, finely chopped
3 carrots, grated
3 cloves garlic, crushed
4 tbsp oil
1 tbsp margarine
1 tbsp paprika
salt
white pepper
pinch nutmeg
bay leaf
parmesan cheese or beaten egg for garnish

In 3 tbsp very hot oil fry 3 onions, garlic and potatoes; add spices and spinach leaves, mixing constantly for 4 minutes. Add the stock and boil for 2 more minutes. Remove from heat and liquidize until it becomes a creamy soup.

Melt the margarine and 1 tbsp oil and fry the remaining onions, carrots, bay leaf and garlic, until soft. Add this to the creamy spinach.

Reheat and serve with parmesan cheese on top or a beaten egg stirred in (as for Sopa Criolla).

Sopa de Lentejas
Lentil and vegetable soup

Chile
serves 6
Vegan (without garnish)

This is a traditional Chilean dish.

350 g (12 oz) green lentils
4 sticks celery, cut in short lengths
3 carrots, cut in round slices
2 tbsp margarine
2 tbsp oil
2 tbsp flour
2 vegetable stock cubes
salt and pepper
grated parmesan cheese or cream and finely chopped parsley to garnish

Cook the lentils with celery and carrots in about 2 l (2½ pints) of water.

Fry onions in half the margarine and oil until they are nearly golden. Mix with the cooked lentils and liquidize. Season.

In a separate pan put the remaining margarine and oil and brown the flour stirring constantly. Add the stock, avoiding lumps. Mix with the blended lentil mixture. Reheat if necessary.

When you serve sprinkle with some grated parmesan cheese and parsley; if you do not have cheese use cream.

Sopa de Platano Verde
Green plantain soup

Venezuela
serves 4
Vegan

This is very quick and easy to prepare.

5 green plantains
120 ml (4 fl oz) oil
2 or 3 vegetable stock cubes

Cut the plantains in round slices and fry in very hot oil, turning them over till they are golden. Make up about 1 l (1¾ pints) stock. Pass the plantains through a sieve or purée in a blender, adding the stock. Simmer for 2 or 3 minutes. Serve hot with cream (optional).

Sopa de Coco
Coconut soup

Venezuela
serves 6

This is a fresh soup and can be served hot or cold. Coconuts are used in a lot of dishes in the northern countries of South America. They grow wild as well as being grown as a crop.

1½ l (2½ pints) vegetable stock, made woth vegetable stock cubes
250 g (9 oz) fresh grated coconut or coconut cream
4 tbsp rice flour or 2 tbsp semolina
275 ml (½ pint) water or milk
2 tbsp cream

Prepare the stock, put on the stove and add the coconut. Cook for 2 minutes. Dissolve the rice flour in water or milk and add to the mixture. Boil for 5 more minutes. Season.

Serve with cream.

Sopa de Zanahoria
Carrot soup

Venezuela
serves 4
Vegan

This is another recipe from my Venezuelan friends.

450 g (1 lb) carrots, diced
2 medium onions, finely chopped
2 vegetable stock cubes
2 tbsp margarine
4 tsp tapioca
1 clove garlic, crushed
2 tsp paprika
1 to 1½ tbsp fresh parsley, finely chopped
salt
pinch white pepper

Fry the onions in the margarine, add crushed garlic, carrots and spices and stir. Dissolve the stock cubes in 1 l (1¾ pints) boiling water and add to the carrot mixture. When the carrots are just soft, liquidize and return to heat. Stir in the tapioca to thicken it and cook for a few more minutes.

Serve garnished with parsley.

Salsa Roja
Maria's red sauce

Chile
Vegan

This is my favourite blended sauce to add to my dishes instead of tomato puree.

450 g (1 lb) fresh tomatoes, chopped
2 big red peppers, cut in strips
2 fresh chillies, chopped very finely
salt and pepper

Put the vegetables in a little water and boil for about 10 minutes. Cool and liquidize. Season. This makes about 425 ml (¾ pint). It can be kept in the fridge or freezer and used as needed in stews and bakes.

Mexican red sauce

Vegan

675 g (1½ lb) fresh tomatoes
2 large red peppers
2 medium onions
3 cloves garlic
3 fresh chillies
½ tsp cumin
pinch black pepper

Cut the tomatoes, peppers and onions into small pieces. Combine all the ingredients in a blender. This sauce keep very well for 2 weeks; keep in a good sealed jar with a little oil on top to preserve.

Salsa Ranchera
Tomato marinade

Mexico
Vegan

450 g (1 lb) firm ripe tomatoes, finely chopped
6 fresh chillies, finely chopped
1 onion, finely chopped
2 cloves garlic, very finely chopped
a generous handful coriander leaves
salt and pepper

Mix all the ingredients and allow to marinate for about 20 minutes before you plan to serve. Use as a fresh filling for tacos or as a topping for tostadas.

Salsa Adobada
Dried chilli sauce

Mexico
Vegan

750 g (1½ lb) fresh ripe tomatoes
6 dried red chillies
1 small onion, chopped
3 or 4 cloves garlic, crushed
4 tbsp oil
salt and pepper

To make a very rich tomato sauce first roast the tomatoes on a griddle, or under a grill, turning often to char the skin all over. Meanwhile soften the chillies in a little boiling water for 2 minutes. Remove tomato skins, then liquidize thoroughly with the other ingredients. A drop of the water in which the chillies were soaked can be added if the sauce is very thick.

Heat the oil until very hot, add the thick sauce and cook for a few minutes.

Salsa de Avocado
Avocado dip

Mexico
serves 6

450 g (1 lb) courgettes, sliced
2 avocados
1 tbsp single cream or strained plain yogurt
pinch black pepper
salt

Steam the courgettes for 3 or 4 minutes, sprinkled with a pinch of salt. They should soften but still be crisp to keep their flavour. Allow to cool.

Skin the avocados at the last minute and liquidize with the courgettes; add the cream or yogurt and black pepper. The sauce should be like double cream; if too thick add a drop of courgette stock.

Use this as a dip or for tacos.

Paltas Rellenas
Stuffed avocado

Chile

serves 4

A very simple dish, make it and enjoy the flavour and the textures.

4 firm ripe medium avocados
2 hard boiled eggs
1 tbsp mayonnaise or soya-based mayonnaise
1 plain lettuce

Mash the hard boiled eggs and mix in the mayonnaise. At the last minute scoop out half the flesh of the avocado and mix with the egg. Then fill the avocados with this mixture.

Serve with lettuce.

Guacamole
Avocado purée

Mexico

serves 4
Vegan

I am very particular about how this is made. Always use ripe avocados, never try to use unripe ones as it will end up being bitter. Follow the instructions exactly; if anything else is added to the recipe – curry, lemon juice, vinegar or anything like that – it becomes an avocado dip and not authentic guacamole. It is very simple but delicious, just so!

2 large ripe avocados
½ bunch coriander, finely chopped (there is no substitute)
4 medium firm tomatoes, finely chopped
3 fresh chillies, finely chopped
salt and pepper
totopos to garnish

Mix the chopped ingredients together at least an hour in advance and keep in a cool place until you need them.

At the last minute cut the avocados in half and mash with a fork. Add to the chopped mixture and season.

Serve in individual small dishes topped with 4 or 5 pieces of totopos.

 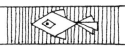

Totopos
Corn tortilla chips

Mexico
Vegan

5 corn tortillas
oil
salt

Cut the tortillas in quarters and deep fry for about 2 minutes until brown and crispy like chips. Drain them and sprinkle with salt. They keep well.

Ají de Aguacate
Avocado starter

Colombia
serves 4
Vegan (if eggs omitted)

This and the other Colombian recipes are from the Altiplano, a mountainous region in central Colombia where traditions are still much kept, dairy products are abundant and the nights are cold in contrast to bright sunny days. They have been given to me by Angela, a dear Colombian friend of the family whom I met in 1977.

2 large avocados, peeled and chopped
juice of 1 lemon
2 hard boiled eggs, chopped or sliced (optional)
Ají de hierbas
2 spring onions, chopped
1 onion, finely chopped
1 large ripe tomato, peeled and chopped
4 chillies, finely chopped
250 ml (1 cup) red or white wine vinegar
2 tbsp fresh coriander, finely chopped
½ tbsp fresh parsley, finely chopped
salt and pepper

Soak the chillies in the vinegar for 30 to 45 minutes so that the vinegar takes the taste of the chillies. Meanwhile chop the other ingredients for the ají de hierbas. Remove the chillies from the vinegar and discard them. Add all the chopped ingredients to the vinegar and stir.

This can be kept in the fridge for several days in a glass container. It is best to use a wooden spoon as the vinegar reacts with metal.

Mix avocado, ½ cup of ají de hierbas, lemon juice and eggs with a wooden spoon and serve in a small glass dish. Keep in a glass bowl in the fridge.

Tomates Rellenos
Stuffed tomatoes

Chile
serves 6

These are quite filling but generally served as a starter. If you want to use them as a main course try to find really big tomatoes, increase the quantities and allow two or three per person and serve with rice and a green salad.

6 beef tomatoes
1 small onion
½ jar mayonnaise, to taste
225 g (8 oz) frozen sweet corn
200 g (7 oz) vegetarian mushroom and herb paté
6 lettuce leaves
2 tbsp parsley, finely chopped
8 medium leaves fresh basil
salt and pepper

Steam the sweet corn with 2 finely chopped leaves of basil (or parsley) for 5 minutes.

Cut a slice 5 cm (2") in diameter off the top of the tomatoes and scoop out the flesh leaving a thin layer of flesh inside. Mix the tomato flesh with the vegetarian paté, mayonnaise, 1 tbsp parsley, sweet corn and seasoning.

Fill the tomatoes with the mixture, using a teaspoon. If you have basil put a leaf on top of each tomato, or sprinkle with parsley.

Serve on top of lettuce.

Other fillings

225 g (8 oz) frozen sweet corn
3 green peppers, finely chopped
1 big mug cooked rice
2 tbsp mayonnaise
salt and pepper

Steam the sweet corn, mix with the other ingredients and the tomato flesh. Season and allow to cool. Fill the tomatoes with the mixture.

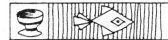

4 *hard boiled eggs*
2 *tbsp mayonnaise*
1 *clove garlic, crushed*
1 *small onion, finely chopped*
2 *tbsp parsley, finely chopped*

Mash the hard boiled eggs and mix with the other ingredients and the tomato flesh. Season. Fill the tomatoes with the mixture.

Huevos Chimbos   *Peru*
Stuffed eggs   serves 6

6 *hard boiled eggs*
250 *g (8 oz) roasted salted peanuts*
2 *tbsp mayonnaise, or soya-based mayonnaise*
1 *plain lettuce*
3 *firm ripe tomatoes*
2 *tbsp fresh parsley, finely chopped*
pepper

Grind the peanuts in a food processor or grinder and mix with the mayonnaise. Season with pepper; no salt is needed as the peanuts are salty.

Cut the eggs in half lengthways. Remove the yolks and mix with the peanuts. Fill the eggs with the mixture.

Serve two halves of filled egg per person, on a bed of lettuce leaves and garnished with tomato and parsley.

Allende is Murdered

What was the atmosphere like? What were the feelings on the day you realised that the coup was actually occurring? How did you first hear about it?

M On the radio the first thing in the morning, on 11th September 1973, the man on the radio said about a coup d'état, and we were angry, we were disappointed, we were extremely sad, very very sad, because we never said, well all these years have been thrown away, we never fall in that. Yes, we were very very sad, very upset, especially when we heard Allende was killed.

When did that happen?

M The same day about 2 o'clock.

Did you know what was happening, because they bombed the palace didn't they? Did you hear that happening? Could you hear gun fire?

M From the house, we hear the bombing.

V We hear the plane but it was far away from our house, and what they say, by about 4 o'clock they say that Allende shot himself, committed suicide.

Did you believe it?

M No one believed.

V Nobody can believe, Allende wasn't the man to kill himself.

M He was a fighter.

V He said he would be there.

Did you hear him on the radio? Did he speak that morning?

M Only one radio station, the station who belong to us, the voice of the people.

V 'This will be my last speech', I think he said, he said that we have to be careful, we have not to be humiliated and he said, 'one day the avenues will open again along which the free can walk', something like that.

Did you go to work that day, Victor?

V No, because there wasn't any transport.

M Everything was controlled by the police in the street and they didn't allow buses or anyone to go to their job and the people very early in the morning who did get the chance to go to their job they had to stop in their places of job.

V Allende went to the palace about 8 o'clock in the morning and he knew, and he reached the palace and he stay there with his personal guard and some people, there were about 40 people altogether. He sent away the guard who would take care of the palace during normal days and he stayed with his own supporters in the main room where they were killed.

They were actually fighting, were they?

V Allende had a machine gun, it was a present from Fidel Castro when he went to Cuba.

M Allende was fighting but he was killed.

V They show one of his doctors on the TV, they put him on to tell the people that Allende commit suicide but when we saw this man talking we didn't, we couldn't, believe it. The man was frightened, nobody believe him, including nobody from the right wing believe that Allende commit suicide,

M But they spread the news anyway.

V because he was a man of honour.

So what were your thoughts immediately after the coup?

V We stayed at home, people from our branch came, massive numbers I have to meet, 15, and I have to send them away because it was so dangerous. They wanted to stay with us, they want to take care of us. I said to them, 'go home, take care of yourselves, we will be caught, if there is something, a new development'. I send some messenger to the party house to see what was going on but their door was closed. We were waiting for an order to go somewhere to pick up the guns, it was an order.

You were saying that the party had said it would arm the workers and the peasants if there was a coup?

V Yes, but that never happened.

Did you ever believe it would?

V I did in the beginning, but when I went to a meeting nearly a month before, I stopped to believe then, because I saw that you cannot, if you are not politically motivated you will not know how to use it, it isn't a question just to give guns to the people just like that.

So were you arguing that you should be trained in how to use them?

V Yes, I told them,'I don't believe you, if you don't provide now I think it will be too late,'and they shut me down.

Was this in the congress or the party?

V It was a big emergency meeting they call. At the beginning there was about 80 people in the meeting and they were telling us what we can do if there is a coup, the radio will put a record with some special song which we will recognise and then we will be prepared to go on to arms.

M It was a slow dance, they said,'the party's going to play this tune and say these sentences,' but the right wing knew first, it was so crazy, it wasn't a secret.

V We were so naive in that instance, there were a lot of people, traitors in our party, in all the parties, some of the people who were infiltrate our organisations later appeared to be one of the torturers. A woman worked as an informer later after she was tortured. I don't blame her, she was brutally tortured. I think they break her and the only way for her was to work with them, to survive as an informer. But some other women prefer to die, they didn't work for the DINA (secret police) and they died in torture, or they were disappeared. These are very difficult situations, it is so difficult to judge

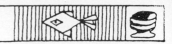

other people when you are under so much pressure, under torture, we are not in the position to condemn anybody.

So what happened in those months between Victor leaving Chile and you managing to leave for Peru? Was it very difficult?

M   Was very bad time. Was very difficult. Apart to be dealing with the family, some of them did not want us to leave, and as well my Raquel got quite ill. She had typhus and she was in hospital. Imagine, it was quite difficult situation without Victor, Raquel in hospital and a lot of pressure and the tension in the country; was really very hard. Was really very hard. I haven't any economic problems, luckily, because Victor left without money and I stayed with all the money we had, all the savings, which wasn't too much but we survived.

Did you feel you were in danger?

M   Well sometimes I felt anything could happen, anytime.

And all the time were there friends of yours, companeros, who were disappearing?

M   I started to hear and to learn about them, some of them. And the political situation was really appalling, was very disgusting at that time.

And did you know what was happening in the stadium?

V   The stadium, like Wembley Stadium. The day of the coup, all sorts of people were put in there. The changing rooms were used as torture chambers.

M   I had quite fresh news from one of the Catholic nuns because she used to go, at four or five in the morning, when she could, to the stadium to find out the whereabouts of the disappeared and the people taken by the military from the area.

So what happened? Was anyone able to get into the stadium then?

M   She was allowed to go in, because she was a sister, she use excuses about taking some medicine.

So she told you what was happening?

M   She told me, yes she told me.

She knew, she knew that people were being tortured and murdered there?

M   Yes, exactly, exactly. Yes and that is the sister Petronila, one of the nuns.

So she is still alive?

M   Yes she is still in Chile, in the same area where we used to live. That woman need to stand in high place, because of her courage she had at that time when the situation was extremely dangerous just to go to the stadium, because she noticed the ferocity and atrocity they were just imposing on the people.

So what was happening to ordinary people after the coup? Did wages go down? Did suddenly lots of goods appear in the shops?

M   Exactly, yes that's what they did a few weeks after the coup, they said everything was normal, the military was using the media quite cleverly, they

say 'everything is normal, we are going to do the best for the country and the goods are all over the country, is no problem, we are going to be providing services and care for people,' which was a lie, absolutely a lie.

So what happened when you were in Peru?

V Well after Maria arrived we start to plan to go somewhere else because the Peruvian government, in the beginning they accept some of the refugees but they didn't give any visas, any permit to stay. I got 90 days visa to stay as a visitor. The Peruvian Chile Committee for Human Rights, they tried to sort it out the possibility to obtain a visa to stay, to have a permit to work as well, but it was impossible.

I put an application in the British Embassy and we spent about 18 months to make success of the application. In the meantime when the visas expire we went to Portugal and we live in Portugal until we obtain the visas. But the visa wasn't obtained easily. The High Commission for the Refugee went to visit us in Portugal, promised to work it out for a visa and was about 10 months and nothing happen, and then we decide to put some pressure on them and we decide to make a hunger strike with three or four more people, including Maria and me. We put the children out of the hunger strike, we told them that we were going to do this thing and they have to take care of the rest of the family, Eduardo and Rodrigo would take care of Victor, Pedro and Raquel. As soon as the strike had start, the second day of the strike, we receive a phone call from Sweden, from the office of the High Commission. They say that they don't accept that sort of method, they don't like pressure, and we said that we were pushed to the decision because we were waiting for so many time and we didn't receive any possible answer and we were sure that if people did a little bit of pressure we would have a good answer soon. The conversation was stopped like that and we followed the strike until the fifth day. During the fifth day we received another call from the United Nations High Commissioner and he promised to intervene if we stoped the hunger strike. We say, 'yes, we will stop if you promise you will act quickly but if you are not, we will give you a week, if you are not even answering in a week we will go ahead again, we are absolutely ready to die if the case is necessary because you can see that it is a matter of urgency. We cannot stay any longer in Portugal because the authorities still have to press us, to put pressure on us to leave the country, but we have nowhere to go '. Well after a week I had a feeling. I told Maria that night, 'Maria, tomorrow somebody is going to call us from the air office telling us that we have our ticket to go to England, our visa and so on'. Next morning about 9.30 we receive a phone call that we have our visas and I have to go to the British Embassy in Lisbon to collect the visa.

V They give us in five days time the ticket and then we were leaving Portugal, and that was the end of our story in transit.

Tell us a little about your time in Portugal.

V   During our year in Portugal we start to do solidarity work with Portuguese supporters and some other Chileans, we start to do some political work against the regime. We receive quite a lot of news through our friends and we manage to mount a campaign to support the Chilean people It was quite successful, we work very very hard for about five or six months doing some publicity, writing documents and printing documents.

Did you have just one room in the hotel, or what, or a room each?

V   Two rooms, one for Maria and Raquel and me, and the other for the boys.

And did they feed you?

V   Yes they paid for our food.

Did you have any money at all?

M   No, and that's another reason why we couldn't send the children to any school,

V   any school for the whole year.

M   And Victor was looking for job, he couldn't find job as well, he was asking, people offered to help and to look for job, no job at all.

V   We did voluntary job in Portugal, it was a political organisation, took over an old palace, not a very big one, and they want to make this palace into a clinic for women who were going to give birth, and they needed to redecorate the place, and we offered with my children and some other children to help them, and we started to work for about three month every single day and that was a good experience. Some people approach to us asking what we need, and sometime we say, well we need probably shoes or trousers or shirt or something, we hadn't many clothes, and people provide some of the clothes for us.

When you came to England, did you know anything about England at all?

V   No we didn't know nothing at all.

V   Well we knew that according to the stereotype that in England most of the people are wearing hat and stick.

M   Umbrella.

V   We were very disappointed when we came to London and didn't see any man with hat and umbrella or stick. Apart from that we didn't know nothing about it.

So what was most surprising about England when you came? Did you come straight to Newcastle?

V   No, we came to London for about 25 days.

M   Can I tell what was my first shock when we arrive in England. They isolate us in a room, the immigration officers,

V   all the family

M   waiting for a doctor to see us. That was my first shock. And the second one, was when they changed my name.

They changed your name?

M   Yes, because in my passport I am Maria Figueroa Zuñiga, married to Victor Fenick, but they just without asking me, they just put Maria Fenick.

V   Later we understand that this is the way, the tradition in this country. You have to understand sometimes the reason why they do it, but there is many way to do the same thing without shocking people.

So what did they do after you got through immigration? Did that take days?

V   No, they did a check of our health and then say, 'you are ready to leave', and then put a stamp in the passport and somebody was waiting for us in the hall,

M   Anita Moselle, from the Chile Solidarity Campaign.

And did you go and stay with her?

V   We went to the Sinclair Hotel, in Shepherd's Bush, which was hired for to keep the Chileans in there.

And how many of you were there, Victor?

V   When we came that night there wasn't more than about twelve people in the hotel.

M   They were waiting for us with a meal, the Chileans, they knew we were, arriving.

Did you get a good welcome?

M   Very nice welcome.

V   Immediately we organise a rota to cook and a couple people have to cook for everybody who was about. The next day there were about thirteen or twelve people living in the hotel and we decide to. But we share the responsibility, it was a very good experience too. Then we were interviewed by the immigration officer who came to the hotel to provide us with the police registration card. He came to give visas, after four years we would have permanent residence. And then we start to make a sort of normal life, we look around London, and waiting for the future accommodation.

Did you have any money at that time?

V   Yes, supplementary benefit, and they took to the office, they talked to the people there, and they ask, 'how many pair of shoes do you have?'. 'Only one', 'and you are wearing one? How many underwear you have?' 'Two, about two'. And they make a list of things and they give, the first money that we receive from the woman as a lump sum, was for Maria and me and Raquel and Pedro and Victor, was about maybe £500. In 1976.

How old were they? How old was Raquel?

V   Raquel was seven.

and how old was Pedro?

V   Pedro was eleven and Victor, thirteen.

and the other two were bigger?

V   Yes, Eduardo was seventeen and Rodrigo, sixteen.

M   But they claimed their own money because they were over 16.

V   And then, well we have to pay for the hotel with the money we receive, we pay the government agency. People start to ask one, 'if you want to stay in London we will try to find a place for you to stay, a house, it is difficult, for London is so overcrowded. If not, we will try to find some other place, do you mind, do you have a special request?' 'No, the only thing we want is a house in which we can start to live again'. And a couple of days, I think it was almost a week, they call us and say, 'there is an offer in Newcastle for a house; do you know something about Newcastle?' 'Yes, I know something about Newcastle, I know there is a chicken disease called Newcastle disease!!!' Well and then we say 'yes, anywhere'. We were told that we had to go to Newcastle because there was a house for us. When they took us to see the house in Throckley one of the clerks went with us and we saw the house, and they say, 'do you like the house?'.

M   Imagine!

V   How are we not going to like it when we have nothing! And we say, 'yes', and then we are organised to move, and the council gave us two weeks to move us.
     And what was your English like at that time? Was that a problem, speaking English?

M   We didn't speak any English.
     What about Eduardo and Rodrigo? Did they speak a little English?

V   No, the English they teach in the school in Chile is so poor, so awful.

M   But you can't believe it, in a few weeks they pick up the language.
     Did they go straight to school?

M   The youngest went first, Pedro and Victor Ludwig and Raquelita.

V   Yes, they went to the school and also they start to make friendship with the children in the area.

M   The first time I have class in English, after 4 years living here. Four years!
     Really? Who organised that? Did you have to do it?

M   It was offered by one of the children's teachers, Mrs Libby Selman. She offered a place in the technical college, Gateshead. She was the one that really help us a lot. Later was a teacher from the Newcastle Polytechnic, Jackie Barry,

V   who is a teacher in the Spanish department, still she work there,

M   and is a good friend of ours.
     Did you feel really isolated when you first came to England and had such difficulty with the language? Was that a very isolating experience?

V   In a way, yes.

M   No, not for me, because my first feeling was, well we have a hard time in Portugal, we have a lot of problems, there was a lot of pressure, and the people were absolutely wonderful and nice, we can't deny that, but the economic situation put us in a very difficult situation; we couldn't manage to take any one of our children to any school, that was really bad for us. And when I arrived here I was really determined to go through whatever it cost

for me I have to go through, I have to deal with the people, I have to listen, I take any advice I could, from friends, about how to cope.

V What I found difficult, was, for me by example, was very hard at the beginning, because I am by nature a man who want to make friends, a man who want to socialise life. And when I saw in my area nobody take notice of us and nobody approach to us to see who are you, to talk in the street with us, I couldn't understand it. The difference for example to go to some place in England you have to be invited, to see some friend you have to be invited, to go on Sunday to have a dinner, a lunch, or something. In Latin America you don't need to be invited, you just go there, say, 'hello, I'm here', and the people say, 'come in, have a glass of wine or some food' and spend the rest of the day with them. That is the way in which we live in Latin America, generally. And I thought that it would be the same here and in every other place. And I was shocked when nobody invite me.

Pastel de Choclo   *Chile*
Vegetable casserole with creamed sweetcorn topping   serves 6
Vegan (if egg omitted)

'Librillo' is Chilean for a special earthenware dish used to cook food in the oven, which is then served in smaller earthenware dishes. These hold the flavour and this is how this dish would be prepared in Chile. This is a dish we have made in the Café for a long time and is really popular. The creamy corn looks and tastes delicious.

Topping
900 g (2 lb) frozen sweet corn, defrosted, or 12 fresh young corn on the cob
2 eggs, hard boiled and sliced (optional)
12 olives (optional)
2 tbsp fresh basil
3 tbsp margarine
2 tbsp corn oil
demerara sugar
salt and pepper
Filling
600 g (1¼ lb) onions, finely sliced
225 g (8 oz) carrots, diced
225 g (8 oz) courgettes, diced; or fresh green beans, sliced
225 g (8 oz) frozen mixed vegetables
4 tbsp oil
1 tsp paprika
salt and pepper

Fry the onions in very hot oil until soft. Meanwhile steam the vegetables. When the onions are done mix with the vegetables, spices and seasoning and cook for a further couple of minutes.

Cream the corn in a food processor or the grinding attachment of a blender until smooth. An ordinary blender is not quite good enough generally to make the corn really smooth. If you don't have a grinding function on your blender you could use a hand operated 'mouli' type grater. If you are using fresh corn you can use the medium grating surface of a hand grater. Anyway, make great efforts to get the corn really smooth; it makes quite a difference. Heat the oil and margarine (it is better to use a mixture as the margarine gets brown and burns more quickly) in a thick bottomed pan; use a heat diffuser, this helps to stop the corn sticking to the pan. Pour in the creamed corn and

cook stirring frequently. It takes about 30 to 35 minutes (not less) for the corn to cook properly. When cooked add the finely chopped basil and seasoning.

Fill an ovenproof dish with the vegetables, add slices of egg and olives (if using) and top with the sweet corn. Sprinkle brown sugar on top and put in a hot oven for about 6 minutes until golden brown.

Serve immediately with tomato or green salad. Most of the corn dishes we serve with tomato salad. This dish is very filling, though you would be tempted by a second bit!

If you like to prepare in advance both the filling and the topping keep well in a freezer.

Pastel Azteca   *Mexico*
Courgette and sweet corn bake   serves 4

Another dish we have introduced to the café which has become popular. We always serve this in individual dishes.

450 g (1 lb) sweet corn
450 g (1 lb) courgettes, diced
350 g (12 oz) onions, finely sliced
225 g (8 oz) tomatoes, chopped
2 to 3 chillies, very finely chopped
225 g (8 oz) cheddar or gouda cheese, grated
4 tbsp single cream
150 ml (¼ pint) sunflower oil
3 tbsp oil for frying tortillas
8 corn tortillas

Steam the sweet corn. Heat the oil and when very hot fry the onion stirring constantly. When nearly transparent add chillies, tomatoes and salt, stirring for 4 minutes more. Then add courgettes, mixing thoroughly. Put the lid on and cook for 3 minutes more; when courgettes are nearly tender add sweet corn, mix well and switch off. If you prepare this dish early or the night before, keep in the fridge.

When ready to serve, heat up the pastel mixture in a pan and place in an oven tray or individual earthenware dishes. Fry the tortillas one by one very quickly in hot oil, about 20 seconds each side. Fold the tortillas in half and place two folded tortillas on each portion. Cover the tortillas with grated cheese and cream. Put in a hot oven for 4 to 5 minutes to melt the cheese.

Lentejas Gratinadas
Lentil and cheese bake

Chile

serves 5– 6

This is my grandmother's recipe; she always made something new and beautiful for me to eat, she was wonderful. All the time, when cooking, she was never in a hurry, she always had the time and willing to treat her family. This has become one of the all time favourites at the Café. It has a delicious thick gravy and the texture of the fried potatoes and the golden cheesy topping make a magnificent combination. We serve it in individual ceramic dishes which is a very pleasing way to receive this dish.

400 g (14 oz) green lentils
450 g (1 lb) onions, finely sliced
500 g (18 oz) fresh tomatoes (or 400 g tin tomatoes and 1 tbsp tomato puree)
400 g (14 oz) potatoes, peeled and diced
100 g (4 oz) cheddar cheese, grated
50 g(2 oz) parmesan cheese
3 tbsp oil
corn oil for frying
75 g (3 oz) breadcrumbs
5 cloves garlic, crushed
2 tsp cumin seeds
1 tbsp fresh parsley or basil
½ tsp oregano
½ tsp white pepper
salt

Put the lentils to cook in cold water with the cumin seeds and simmer for 25 to 30 minutes, adding salt half way through.

In another pan heat the oil until very hot, add the onions and crushed garlic and fry for about 3 minutes. Then add finely chopped tomatoes and the basil or parsley. After 5 minutes, add oregano, pinch of salt and white pepper.

Mix together the lentils, the fried ingredients, parmesan cheese and breadcrumbs, arriving at a thick but not dry consistency.

Deep fry the potatoes.

Fill an oven dish ¾ full with the ready heated lentils. Then add a layer of diced fried potatoes with a generous sprinkling of grated cheese and pop into a hot oven for 5 to 10 minutes.

Serve with a light salad.

Tomatican
Rich tomato stew

Chile

serves 6
Vegan

This is a lovely rich tomato stew full of colour. It is much better made with fresh tomatoes for their flavour. It looks most attractive on a bed of white rice as it would be eaten in Chile. Traditionally, this is prepared with meat, but generally people prepare it without meat.

350 g (12 oz) frozen sweet corn
225 g (8 oz) green beans, cut in short lengths
1 kg (2¼ lb) fresh tomatoes
350 g (12 oz) potatoes, diced
225 g (8 oz) carrots, diced
2 large onions, finely chopped
½ bulb garlic, crushed
1 red pepper, chopped
oil for deep frying
2 tbsp fresh basil
2 tbsp fresh parsley
¼ tsp cumin
½ tsp paprika
salt and pepper

Heat some of the oil and fry onions, garlic, tomatoes and red pepper until softened. Add the herbs and spices and continue frying for 1 minute, stirring constantly.

Meanwhile steam the sweetcorn, green beans and carrots until tender; and in a deep frying pan fry potatoes.

Mix vegetables, potatoes and tomato mixture.

Serve on a bed of rice with green peas.

Croquetas de Garbanzos en Salsa de Vino *Chile*
Chick pea croquettes in wine and tomato sauce *serves 4*

These are crispy and golden on the outside and soft inside; a nice combination of textures and lovely with the wine sauce. This is a traditional Chilean dish which I have added to and improved.

225 g (8 oz) chick peas, soaked overnight
900 g (2 lb) fresh ripe tomatoes, quartered
100 g (4 oz) carrot, grated
2 large red peppers, seeded and cut into thick slices
75 ml (3 fl oz) dry white wine
3 medium onions, finely chopped
4 small cloves garlic, crushed
3 tbsp plain wholewheat flour
1 egg
½ cup breadcrumbs
3 bay leaves
3 tbsp fresh parsley, finely chopped
½ tsp cumin seeds
pinch of oregano
oil for frying
salt

Cover chick peas with about 8 cm (3″) water and cook in a pressure cooker with cumin seeds and salt for 25 minutes; alternatively boil with cumin seeds for 20 minutes, then add salt and continue boiling for 25 minutes more. As the chick peas cook, prepare the sauce.

Fry the onions in very hot oil till transparent, adding garlic and bay leaves half way through. Then add 550 g (20 oz) tomatoes and 2 tbsp parsley and cook till the tomatoes are well done. Add oregano.

Make a sauce by boiling the peppers and 350 g (12 oz) tomatoes in a small amount of water, just enough to cover them, for 10 minutes. Set aside and liquidize when cool.

Combine this with the onion and tomato mixture and add wine.

When the chick peas are cooked quite soft and very little liquid remains, purée or mash them, until like mashed potatoes. Check if salt is needed. Beat the egg, add breadcrumbs and 2 tsp flour and mix with chick peas. Form into balls the size of ping-pong balls, using remaining flour to prevent your

hands getting sticky. Roll them in the carrot and remaining parsley and deep fry till they are golden brown.

Serve on a bed of rice with the sauce poured over the top. Acccompany with a green salad.

Estofado de Garbanzos
Chick pea stew

Chile
serves 6
Vegan

In Chile traditionally we cook chick peas with cabbage and rice but all sorts of things, pumpkin and many other variations, could be added. This is my husband Victor's recipe, which has been improved and added to during our time at the Red Herring.

350 g (12 oz) chick peas, soaked overnight
350 g (12 oz) courgettes, sliced
350 g (12 oz) white cabbage, finely chopped
225 g (8 oz) frozen sweetcorn
200 g (7 oz) carrots, in thin round slices
100 g (4 oz) green beans or peas, fresh or frozen
2 onions, finely chopped
3 cloves garlic, crushed
2 tsp sweet paprika
1 tsp cumin seeds
½ tsp oregano
2 tsp salt

Drain and rinse the chick peas and put in cold water with cumin seeds. Bring to the boil and cook them for 50 minutes or more till they are tender. Halfway through add salt. Do not overwater them. Keep cooking water which has become thick.

Fry onions and carrots in very hot oil until onions are transparent; add chopped cabbage, spices and garlic and fry for 4 more minutes.

Steam the other vegetables until tender and mix with the cooked chick peas and onions. Check the seasoning.

It is good to prepare this dish the night before or early. I found it more tasty when it is prepared the day before and kept in the fridge.

Serve with rice or salad.

Pastel de Garbanzos con Salsa Roja y Repollo *Chile*
Vegan

Chick peas with vegetables, red sauce and spicy cabbage   serves 6

This is a dish I made up one day with various leftovers. Always of course we are looking for ways to use leftovers so as not to waste anything. This worked very well and I'm happy to share it with you.

450 g (1 lb) chick peas, soaked overnight
350 g (12 oz) onions, finely chopped
450 g (1 lb) carrots, sweet corn, broccoli and peas
3 cloves garlic, crushed
2 large or 3 medium red peppers, seeded and sliced
half a medium white or savoy cabbage, finely sliced
red sauce, made with 200 g (8 oz) tomatoes
7 tbsp oil
½ tsp cumin seeds
1 tsp paprika
1 tsp coarse pepper
salt

Rinse the chick peas and put in 1¾ l (3½ pints) cold water. Bring to the boil, add cumin seeds and after boiling for 5 minutes add 2 tsp salt. Cook for about 55 minutes till soft. Do not drain. Mash to make a creamy puree.

Steam the carrots, sweetcorn, broccoli and peas.

Heat 4 tbsp oil and fry onions and garlic. When soft add the steamed vegetables, seasoning and half the red sauce.

Fry the cabbage in the remaining oil. Add paprika and pepper and continue stirring until nearly soft.

Put the fried onion and vegetable mixture in an oven tray or individual dishes, then add a layer of mashed chick peas and a layer of spicy cabbage. Finish with the remaining red sauce.

Put in a hot oven for 5 minutes and serve with salad.

Estofado de Papas

Potato stew with pickling onions and chestnuts

Chile

serves 6
Vegan

This is a traditional Chilean dish often made with beef or fish fillets. I added the mushrooms and the red sauce.

450 g (1 lb) pickling onions, peeled, whole
450 g (1 lb) small even new potatoes, whole
365 g (12 oz) dried chestnuts, soaked overnight
225 g (8 oz) button mushrooms, whole
1 big red pepper sliced
6 to 7 cloves garlic, crushed
75 g (3 tbsp) margarine
575 ml (1 pint) fresh vegetable stock
200 ml (8 fl oz) dry white wine
6 tbsp red sauce
3 tbsp fresh parsley, finely chopped
2 bay leaves
½ tsp sweet paprika
salt and pepper.

Melt the margarine and fry the crushed garlic and onions for about 8 minutes, then add the bay leaves, peppers and seasoning. Add wine, paprika then mushrooms. After 2 minutes switch off.

Cook chestnuts in water for 50–60 minutes. In a separate pan slowly cook the potatoes in the stock. When soft add them to the onions and mix in the chestnuts; try not to spoil the shapes when you mix them. Add parsley and red sauce.

Serve hot in a deep plate with steamed broccoli or any vegetable you like best.

Pastel del Hongos
Aubergine and mushroom bake

Venezuela
serves 4

This is a traditional Venezuelan dish. It was first prepared for me by a Venezuelan friend, Carmen, whom I met in Newcastle in 1976!

2 large aubergines, finely sliced
480 g (1 lb) mushrooms, finely sliced
1 large onion, finely chopped
2 cloves garlic, crushed
2 tbsp red sauce
5 tbsp dry white wine
100 g (4 oz) bread crumbs
50 g (2 oz) parmesan
100 g (4 oz) cheddar cheese
2 eggs, beaten
3 tbsp margarine or oil
1 tbsp fresh parsley, chopped
1 tbsp fresh basil
pinch of cinnamon
½ tsp black pepper
For white sauce
2 tbsp butter or margarine
2 tbsp 85% flour
275 ml (½ pint) milk
2 egg yolks

Lightly salt and brush oil on the top of the aubergine slices and put in a medium oven until soft and golden.

Saute the onions and garlic in oil or margarine until soft, then add the mushrooms. Add red sauce, parsley, cinnamon, black pepper and wine to the mushrooms. Boil until the juice is absorbed. Then add bread crumbs, beaten eggs and parmesan cheese. Mix thoroughly and remove from heat. This could be prepared in advance, it keeps well in the fridge.

Make a white sauce by melting the butter or margarine. Then stir in the flour and cook for 2 or 3 minutes. Add milk, whisking to avoid lumps. Remove from heat and whisk in egg yolks.

In an ovenproof dish first put a layer of aubergine, then half of the mushroom sauce, a layer of aubergine and cover with the rest of the mushroom sauce. Cover this with white sauce and sprinkle with the rest of the cheese. Bake in a moderate oven (gas 5 or 350°) for 30 minutes covered, then 10 minutes uncovered.

Serve immediately with cooked rice and fresh salad.

Papas a la Huancaina   *Peru*
Potatoes with cheese and peanut sauce   serves 6

This is a Peruvian dish of cooked potatoes served cold on a bed of lettuce and topped with a very rich sauce of cheese, peanuts and spices. I first discovered this when I was in exile in Peru where some friends prepared it for us. Although this may sound a little unexciting it both looks and tastes very special; it has become very popular in the Café. Using red lettuce or endive adds something to the appearance too.

9 small to medium sized salad potatoes
1 plain lettuce
1 tbsp finely choped parsley, or paprika, to garnish
For the sauce
100 g (4 oz) plain yogurt
150 g (5 oz) mayonnaise or soya-based mayonnaise
50 g (2 oz) chilli paste
250 g (9 oz) salted peanuts
200 g (7 oz) crumbly white cheese, e.g. Wensleydale or Lancashire, grated

Wash and boil the potatoes whole until tender and leave to cool.

Grind the peanuts finely in a food processor or blender. First liquidize the nuts, cheese, yoghurt, mayonnaise and chilli sauce together and put it all through the blender again; the sauce must be a thick creamy consistency.

Arrange potato halves on a bed of lettuce, spoon some sauce onto the potato halves and garnish with parsley or paprika.

Serve with a portion of green salad and a mound of rice salad or cooked rice.

Empanadas

Chile
serves 12
Vegan (if eggs omitted)

It is the empanadas which we first made for sale to people on Tyneside and their popularity is enduring. We always provide them at concerts and other events. They are delicious and so easy to eat in the hand, ideal for picnics and packed lunches. Their appearance is very attractive and to get them like the one in the photograph requires a little practice but they are pretty straightforward. These are the all-time favourite.

Filling
900 g (2 lb) onions, finely chopped
100 g (4 oz) fresh peas
100 g (4 oz) fresh broad beans
150 g (6 oz) fresh green beans } OR *450 g (1 lb) mixed vegetables*
cut in short lengths [2 cm (¾")]
100 g (4 oz) carrots
75 g (3 oz) sultanas, soaked in hot water
2 hard boiled eggs, sliced (optional)
12 green or black olives, stoned
125 ml (¼ pint) corn oil
1 egg, beaten or soya milk, to glaze
2 tsp cumin seeds
2 tsp sweet paprika
½ tsp chilli powder
salt
Dough
675 g (1½ lb) plain flour
100 g (4 oz) vegetarian fat
275 ml (½ pint) boiling water
1 tsp salt

In a thick bottomed pan heat the oil; when very hot fry the onions for 8 minutes until transparent. Add the spices and remove from the heat.

Steam the vegetables and when cooked mix with the onions, add salt and pepper. Rinse the sultanas (this makes them less sweet) and add them.

Melt the fat and whilst still hot add to the flour and add salt and boiling water, mixing constantly to achieve a firm dough. Do **not** knead; leave to cool.

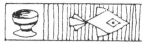

Divide the dough into 12 equal balls, dust the surface of the table with flour and roll each ball into circles 20 cm (8") in diameter.

Place 1 heaped tbsp of the filling on the top half of the circle of dough. Share out the olives and egg so you put some on top of each filling. Brush the bottom edge with cold water and fold the bottom half over. Press to seal, wet the edge again and fold back towards the filling so that the edge is an even margin of dough about 1 cm (½") wide and 4 layers of dough thick. This is then crimped with a thumb and forefinger to create the distinctive pattern around the sealed edge. Be very bold with the crimping so the pattern is conspicuous; after you have done a few you will get the hang of it and they will look very attractive. Brush the top with beaten egg, or for vegan empanadas, soya milk.

Bake in a very hot oven for about 15 to 20 minutes.

Serve hot or cold as a full meal with a mixed salad or as a snack.

Porotos con Mazamorra

Chile

Thick bean and sweet corn stew

serves 4
Vegan

In central America beans are called frijoles but in South America all beans are called porotos. This is a traditional dish, made only in Chile. Mazamorra is Chilean for 'a mess' but here it means 'opaque', i.e. the stew is not clear.

250 g (9 oz) white kidney beans or flageolot beans, soaked overnight
450 g (1 lb) frozen sweetcorn, defrosted 2 to 3 hours in advance
180 g (6 oz) yellow pumpkin, halved
1 medium onion, finely chopped
3 tbsp margarine or corn oil
2 cloves garlic, crushed
2 tsp sweet paprika
2 tsp fresh basil, finely chopped
½ tsp cumin seeds
salt and pepper

Drain and rinse the beans thoroughly. Bring them to the boil in 2 l of fresh water with the cumin seeds. After boiling rapidly for 10 minutes add the two pieces of pumpkin and salt. Simmer until the pumpkin is soft, then take it out, mash and put aside.

In the meantime cream the sweet corn in a food processor or the grinder of a blender until smooth. Heat the oil or margarine in a thick bottomed pan, add the creamed corn and cook for 30-35 minutes, stirring frequently to stop the corn sticking. Then add the beans and fresh basil. Cook for an extra 10 minutes on low heat, then add the mashed pumpkin. In a separate pan fry the onions in oil with the paprika and seasoning. Add to the cooked beans and creamed corn.

Serve hot, with tomato salad on a separate small plate.

Papas Chorreadas   *Colombia*
Coated potatoes

1.35 kg (3 lb) medium potatoes, peeled
4 bunches spring onions, finely chopped
3 large ripe tomatoes, finely chopped
275 g (10 oz) cheddar cheese, grated
150 ml (6 oz) double cream
2 tbsp oil
½ tsp cumin
½ tsp salt
½ tsp pepper

Cook the potatoes in salted water until tender.

Meantime heat the oil and fry onions and tomatoes until soft. Add cheese, spices, salt and cream.

Put the potatoes on a serving dish and pour the creamy sauce over.

Serve hot.

Papas a la Cerveza   *Nicaragua*
Potatoes with beer   serves 4
                                                  Vegan

This is a very unusual and different dish. I had it is Nicaragua where it is sold on the street.

450 g (1 lb) potatoes, scrubbed but not peeled
275 ml (½ pint) beer
3 medium beetroots
2 medium onions, finely chopped
1 lemon

Boil potatoes in the skin. When cooked, cool and peel them, dice and them them with the beer and salt on the stove for about 2 minutes, then take off the heat.

In a separate pan, cover the beetroots with water and cook. Then peel and dice them. Mix beetroot with potatoes, add lemon juice and onion.

This should be served hot or cold, with raw cabbage cut into fine strips and with bananas cut lengthways and fried and then used to garnish the cabbage.

Aspilleras

Embroidery in coloured wools is an old craft practised in Chile and the women seem to have adapted the idea to the materials they could get hold of. Some of the patchworks made after the military took power from Allende's government in 1973 were made by women in prison, others by wives or mothers of prisoners protesting about the disappearance or the detention of the men. Now the patchworks are made mostly in workshops of twenty or so women who pool their resources and sell their work, mainly through the churches.

The pictures on the following pages show some of the aspilleras I have made while I have been in Newcastle.

This stands for Latin American women in their struggle through the centuries against repression, against the status quo. We have outstanding women all over Latin America who have been giving their lives for justice and peace.

The woman kneeling is hoping for information about the whereabouts of her husband or son. The Committee for the Relatives of the Disappeared estimate there are 2,500 missing, disappeared, people.

There are still about 500 political prisoners through the country. They wait not knowing when they will get a trial and knowing it may not be a fair one.

Arroz a la Jardinera
Garden rice

Chile

serves 6

Vegan (if egg omitted)

My mother made this dish which is lovely and colourful and can be served
either hot or cold.

300 g (11 oz) long grain rice
400 g (14 oz) potatoes, diced
225 g (8 oz) peas 225 g (8 oz) sweetcorn
2 red peppers, diced
1 green pepper, diced
3 medium onions, very finely chopped
2 cloves garlic, crushed
8 tbsp corn oil
2 tbsp olive oil
oil for deep frying
3 tbsp parsley, finely chopped
3 hard boiled eggs, sliced ⎫
3 tomatoes, sliced   ⎭ *to garnish*
salt and pepper

Fry the rice in half the corn oil for 7 or 8 minutes, stirring constantly to avoid
sticking; turn the heat down if necessary. Add the garlic in the last 2 minutes.
Add 1 l (1¾ pints) boiling water and 2 tsp salt. Cover and simmer until done;
the rice is nicer when the grain is kept whole and not sticky – it may need a
little more water.

Meanwhile steam the sweetcorn and peas. Fry the onions and peppers in the
remaining corn oil until transparent. Season well. Deep fry the potato cubes.

When the rice is cooked stir in the olive oil and the cooked vegetables, and
fried potatoes, then add fresh parsley.

Serve cold in a mound surrounded by alternate slices of fresh tomato and
hard boiled egg, or hot with fried or scrambled eggs.

I improved this dish by adding peas and peppers. Traditionally in my
country it is served with meat, but my mother made this vegetarian version
which is lovely.

Enchiladas

Mexico
serves 4

An enchilada is very particular! Tortillas are a kind of thin, round, flat, unleavened bread which are very versatile and can be used in a variety of ways. The enchilada is a corn tortilla fried and folded with a cheese filling and served with piping hot sauce. This is **the** authentic enchilada: crisp and hot and delicious.

12 corn tortillas
300 g (11 oz) cheddar cheese, grated
1 kg (2¼ lb) fresh tomatoes
1 large onion, very finely chopped
1 red pepper
4 small chillies
2 tbsp fresh coriander
oil for frying

Wash tomatoes, chillis and red pepper in warm water and then boil them for 3 minutes, in just enough water to cover. Cool and liquidize and season with salt and pepper.

Mix the grated cheese with very finely chopped onion.

Reheat the sauce and have it and the cheese to hand. Heat the oil and shallow fry tortillas for about 20 seconds or less on each side. When frying the tortillas, drop them in the oil one at a time; after a few seconds it will start bubbling up, then flip it over quickly and when the second side begins to bubble whip it out, cover half with cheese filling, fold over and repeat with other tortillas as quickly as possible. Serve immediately or keep hot but serve as soon as possible.

Arrange 3 tortillas in a fan shape on each plate, pour over some piping hot sauce and serve with a dollop of refritos and green salad.

LEVÁNTATE Y MIRA LA MONTAÑA... Chile

TALLER KUPAN

This is about a song written by Victor Jara which said 'stand up everybody and look to the mountain from where the sun and the air and wind are coming to us'. The authorities broke his hands so he could not play and then killed him.

Chile

This is the chain restricting our liberty. One day we will break through but there is still a long way to go.

This is about the May Day which is a day involving all the working people all over the world. It depicts a chain of solidarity.

This is a collective farm, something we experienced during Allende's government. It was a lovely experience, it could happen again some time; I hope so!

Refritos
Refried beans

Mexico
serves 6 to 8
Vegan

These can be used in many dishes and are a staple in many countries in Latin America. They can be added as a side dish to almost any other dish, particularly if the other dish is needing some protein or to convert a snack to a wholesome meal.

500 g (18 oz) pinto or rosecoco beans, soaked overnight
1 medium onion, coarsely chopped
3 cloves garlic, crushed
oil
1 tsp black pepper
2 tsp salt

Pick over and wash the beans in several changes of water. Drain and place in a large saucepan with the onions, garlic and pepper. Add enough cold water to cover by 4 cms (1½") and bring to the boil. Cover and after 5 minutes add the salt and cook for another 30 minutes or so until the beans are tender. Do not drain, there should not be much liquid left. Mash them and put aside until needed.

Heat a little oil in a saucepan and refry the beans, mashing and stirring them constantly to avoid sticking and to achieve a creamy texture.

Refritos will keep for 4 or 5 days in the fridge. Add more oil when reheating; this makes them even creamier. They get more delicious the long you keep refrying them.

Tacos

Mexico
serves 6
Vegan

Tacos are another way of using tortillas in which the tortilla is spread with a filling and very carefully rolled up and fried in hot oil. We often serve them in the Café, usually with a green salad and a little refritos on the side and a sauce; they are always popular.

Allow 3 tacos per person. Two different fillings are given below and you can also use refritos. You can of course fill each tacos with a different filling for greater variety and excitement – use any combination!

Make the tacos by placing 1 tbsp of filling on a tortilla and very carefully rolling it up. Fry in hot oil with the joint downwards to seal it first then turn over, pressing very gently to keep the round shape. Repeat with all the tacos.

Fillings for tacos:

Potato and tomato

450 g (1 lb) potatoes, diced
450 g (1 lb) fresh tomatoes, sliced
450 g (1 lb) onions, finely sliced
4 fresh green chillies, finely chopped
125 ml (¼ pint) oil
½ tsp oregano
salt and pepper

Deep fry the potatoes until cooked and brown. In very hot oil fry the onions until soft, then add the tomatoes, chillies, oregano and seasoning. Cook a little longer and then remove from the heat and mix with the potatoes.

This may be prepared in advance or the day before.

Rajas

6–8 large red or green peppers
350 g (12 oz) onions, finely sliced
250 g (½ lb) fresh tomatoes, sliced
4 fresh green chillies, finely chopped
2 cloves garlic, crushed
oil for frying
salt and pepper

Skin the peppers by charring on a hot griddle or under the grill, turning them over and over until evenly roasted. Place in a plastic bag and cover with a tea towel and leave for 10 or 15 minutes to loosen the skins.

Meanwhile fry the onions, tomatoes, chillies and garlic until soft.

Remove the peppers from the bag one at a time and peel them; the skins should come off very easily now. Remove the stalks and seeds and cut the flesh into strips. Add to the onion mixture and season.

The Red Herring Workers' Co-operative

Nigel, Gwen, Andy, Fiona, Victor, Maria, Meg, Matthew and Jane; members of the Red Herring Workers' Co-operative in August 1990, outside their café and shop.

Chiles Asados con Salsa
Peppers stuffed with cheese in tomato sauce

Mexico
serves 6

All the Mexican recipes were introduced to me by Patricia Rodriquez from Torreon in north east Mexico. She came to Newcastle in 1986 because her husband Francisco was studying at the university. I met her at a friend's just after she arrived and quite soon after she became involved with the Latin American Women's Group. She taught us how to cook Mexican food, especially the most wonderful carrot cake. She introduced these recipes to the Red Herring which helped our Latin American menu very much.

6 green or red peppers (choose big ones with a thick flesh and very healthy)
750–800 g (1½–2 lb) fresh tomatoes
200 g (7 oz) cheddar cheese, grated
3 eggs
1 medium onion, finely chopped
6 dried chillies, finely chopped
oil for frying
pinch oregano

Place the peppers on a hot griddle or under a hot grill, turning them around, taking care not to pinch them. It takes a while to have evenly roasted pepper, without burning them.* Place them in a plastic bag, cover with a tea towel and leave for about 15 to 20 minutes. Meantime prepare the sauce.

Roast the tomatoes under the grill to peel the skin off. Then mash them and mix with the chillies, onion, salt, oregano and a little water. This is not a thick sauce. Keep hot.

Separate the eggs and beat the egg white until firm; then fold in the yolks. Remove one by one the peppers from the plastic bag. Peel the skins off the peppers, it takes time. Make a small slit and take out seeds. Fill the peppers with the cheese and close the slit with a cocktail stick. Then dip in the beaten egg and deep fry over a low flame to avoid them burning. Place on kitchen paper to absorb the oil. Pour the hot sauce over the peppers.

Serve hot with rice, green salad or refritos. Another good way to serve this is with a Mexican style salad made with finely sliced cucumber, chopped oranges, finely chopped fresh chillies, salt and oil. This is how Patricia taught it to me.

* This is the best and authentic old method to keep the wonderful flavour of the peppers. It is not the same if you boil them.

Chiles Rellenos
Mexico

Peppers stuffed with refried beans and coriander
serves 6
Vegan (if cream omitted)

This is another recipe from Patricia. She and Francisco returned to Mexico recently but continue to send us recipes and encouragement. Their support and friendship mean so much to us, they will always be with us in our hearts.

6 green or red peppers
2 onions, finely chopped
½ bunch fresh coriander, finely chopped
2 fresh green chillies, finely chopped
1 small tub of double cream
refritos made with 300 g (11 oz) beans
oil for frying
Mexican red sauce

Roast and peel the peppers using the same method as in Chiles Asados.

Fry the onions and mix with the refritos, coriander and chillies.

Fill the peppers with this mixture taking care to keep their shape; keep warm in a warm oven until ready to serve. Dribble cream (if using) over the top.

Serve with rice with tomatoes, salad and a little Mexican red sauce (optional).

Tostadas
Mexico

Deep fried tortillas with refritos and avocado topping

serves 6

Vegan (if cream omitted)

Of all Mexican food this is one of my favourites, tasty and most attractive. Very rich and nutritious.

18 corn tortillas
3 big ripe avocados
refritos made with 500 g (18 oz) pinto beans
1 plain lettuce, finely shredded, or very finely shredded cabbage
3 medium tomatoes, sliced
1 medium onion, cut in fine round slices
150 g (5 oz) carton single cream (optional)
200 ml (7 fl oz) sunflower oil

Heat the oil in a big pan and when very hot deep fry each tortilla, patting them down gently to avoid the edges curling up; they must be flat. Keep them in a tray on kitchen paper. This can be done in advance, a couple of hours or even days before you need them, if they are kept in a cool airy place.

Mash the avocados.

Spread a thick layer of refritos on each tortilla, then top with mashed avocado, lettuce, onion rings, a generous dollop of cream, and season. Garnish with a slice of tomato.

Place three tostadas on each plate and serve with any sauce you like.

Sopa Seca de Tortilla
Tortilla hotpot

Mexico
serves 4

500 ml (¾ pint) vegetable stock
1 medium onion, finely chopped
1 to 2 cloves garlic, crushed
3 tbsp fresh peeled tomato, crushed
50 g (2 oz) parmesan cheese
4 tbsp corn oil
1 tsp parsley, chopped
2 tbsp fresh coriander
1 tsp mild chilli powder
salt and pepper
6 corn tortillas, cut in fine strips

Heat the vegetable stock and soak coriander in it. Then strain and keep stock.

In a separate pan lightly fry tortillas and drain on kitchen paper. In the same pan fry onions and garlic till transparent, then add tomato, parsley and the spices and salt. Pour the stock into the mixture, add tortilla strips and simmer on a medium heat until thick. Check it does not burn.

Serve hot sprinkled with parmesan cheese with steamed vegetables or cooked potatoes.

Life in Newcastle

So when you settled into Throckley then, did you know that there were a lot of other Latin American people in Newcastle?

V   Yes, while we were waiting for the housing in Throckley we start to have meeting with the rest of the Chilean community, to talk about what we were going to do and how we are going to do some political job,

M   Organise the May Day.

V   solidarity work. We start to organise thing, we print a pamphlet. I wish to have one of the pamphlet that we print in English. Can you imagine the many mistake we make in the pamphlet writing in English, nobody knows how. Veronica help us. And we went to the May Day demonstration. We didn't know where the march was going to start but we met them in the Central Station in 1976 and we joined them, a very short demonstration, a very poor demonstration actually, but we joined them and we followed them and we started to distribute our pamphlet and tried to talk with the cameras, even with our poor language. It was amazing, we were so naive, so naive.

M   No, I don't think it was naive, Victor, it was inexperience.

V   Yes, because for the May Day, in Chile, before the coup it was something. Easily you have half a million people in the Square in Santiago, for that day, easy. Even with the military, we tried to do them and we did.

M   Even after the coup, yes. The trade union in exile organised a column of people from that place. The carabineros and the military stop that column but immediately appear another one in another place; it was organised like that and it was all over Santiago. It was great, great.

V   The whole country was demonstrating.

M   And very proud to say the first big demonstration was in 1978 for International Women's Day; that was the biggest since the coup.

So from the first May Day did you meet people here who were sympathetic and supported you?

V   Yes, quite a lot of people who I don't remember all of the names but I can mention some of the people. Steve Manchee, he was one of the men who was on the committee, Jan Doby,

M   she is still very active and very supportive.

V   and also there is a short man who used to come here to the Red Herring. Charlie, he was on that committee at that time. He was very supportive as well with our people, the people who give shelter at the beginning, how call we the French teacher?

M   David

V   David Place, I think he is head of the French department now; with his wife and a little girl. Quite a lot of people work giving support and they start to give some guide or some advice. But we set up our organisation very soon.

What was that, Victor?

V A sort of Chile committee.

How many Chileans were there in Newcastle?

M Counting the children, 54 to 56.

V About 50, something like that with children, but adults about 25. We start to develop strategies to deal with the problems, how we are going to help our people in Chile, how we are going to do many demonstrations and so on, and we were very successful to do that.

What did you do? What sort of things?

V Well we start to do for example cultural events to show the people of Newcastle our culture.

Was that where Maria's patchworks came in?

M Yes, it was about 1977, I think.

V Maria, I think it very important to mention that through our friend Rose, the wife of the French teacher in the University, they put in contact with the Catholic chaplaincy. And we talk with them, we talked about the problems of the children in the area which we leave, people who have nothing to eat and so on and they decide to establish support for a soup kitchen in the area in which we used to live. That was in '76, and they are still supporting after all these years, they are still supporting.

M And Bob Spence, such a lovely, lovely, lovely man, so cheerful, so understanding. With him we organise the Chile lunches at the Catholic chaplaincy, and we created a Chile committee to have lunches every Wednesday.

V That thing was very, very important; to have this close link with the students of the Catholic chaplaincy, and some of the young people are still coming here to see us. They are really very nice people and did quite a lot of thing to collect money to send every month, including in the summer time, when they were not going to the Poly, or the University, they do some jumble sale or some activities to keep going on, to send this money to the soup kitchen in Chile, and one of the thing we are very proud of it the activities of the students for they are how we can help.

It's great they've kept going on so long, it's remarkable.

V Remarkable, remarkable that still they are doing this every Wednesday; lunch for Chile!

M There was lunch at the Catholic chaplaincy with the students, and suddenly came to my mind that they are supporting a soup kitchen, why not make a patchwork of a soup kitchen; and I made that, that was the first one, and after that someone saw in the lunch the tapestry when we give it to the priest, and we had order for two more, oh we were over the moon, imagine!

You made it as an order for the Catholic chaplaincy?

M A present for the chaplaincy, yes,
and somebody saw it

M but they gave money for the group. We didn't want that money, we put in the funds.

V   Another event that we make here was more in the way to bring our culture to the people of Newcastle, not only the Chilean culture but also the Latin American culture. Whenever we can for example we bring groups from El Salvador, from Nicaragua, from Cuba, from Bolivia and Chile, and also musicians who were in exile as well, like the group 'Karaxu' who came here and played at St Thomas' Church, and also the theatre group, a Chilean popular theatre group who were in exile here, and we showed them for the first time in the Boilermakers' Club in Gateshead and it was packed, packed, and it was a very powerful play because one of the actor has to interpret a man who was tortured.

How was it received, Victor, though?

V   Very well, it was very powerful.

M   The play was good, absolutely wonderful. I think the main reason was because most of the people who were in the popular theatre acting that day, most of them had been in jail.

V   They were, they had been political prisoners.

M   All of them. Especially one of the actors, a woman called Coca Rudolphi. She is in Chile now, but she was really badly treated.

V   She was tortured, raped probably, psychologically tortured.

M   Absolutely, and she did magnificently in the play, very powerful, wonderful.

V   And Hugo as well who was in jail for three or four years, he was beaten and tortured, he received electric shocks very often.

And did you start doing food at those events?

V   In the Boilermakers no, we didn't serve food at that time. It was the first concert when we started the food. It was quite an experience because we were planning to serve Chilean food and nobody know what we can do it at that time, and suddenly someone suggest, 'well what was the most popular food in Chile'? 'Empanadas of course', somebody say, 'empanadas'. So okay we are going to make empanadas. 'Who knows how to make empanadas?' Nobody knows!

M   Well I knew but I didn't want to.

V   So we started to look for the recipe. So what is it empanadas got in? Well, mince meat, fried onion and spices, sultanas, eggs, olives, and because we knew how to make bread it wasn't too much difficult to make a dough, you know, but to fill it and the shape. Maria was more expert because I didn't cook before in my life, very very rarely, I start to cook when I came to England. And Maria start to do the empanadas and we start to follow, to do the shape and so on and we haven't a good cooker like the ones we have now, it was a small one, and we said, 'well, how many empanadas can we make?' A hundred, no that's too little, two hundred, still we would be short, three hundred. And we decide to make three hundred and we did, we spent three days. A bit crazy!

Who did it Victor, you and the family?

V and some of the other Chileans who were there as well. It was amazing making 300 empanadas in this tiny little kitchen.

In your kitchen.

V Yes. So we went to the concert and we nearly nearly sold out.

So that was the Karaxu concert, the first concert that you organised. Good experience.

M The first concert was Karaxu.

And was that at St Thomas' Church?

M Yes, at St Thomas's.

And which year was that?

M 1979.

V Well another thing was very very important apart from the different concerts. In 1978 I think it was, we hear that the relatives of the disappeared launch a hunger strike in Chile and we receive the news and we have a short meeting at home and we decide to call the Chilean committee here to follow the example of our people in Chile and to launch a hunger strike in Newcastle, in England. We decide and we start to look for a place to do it, and someone mention St Thomas' Church, and we went there to talk with the priest in charge, with Ian Harker, and we ask if he could provide the church for us. And he said, 'yes!' and he provided the church for us and we launched the strike, to take nine days, in which we were all involved. They didn't allow me to join the hunger strike because I was suffering from ulcers, but the rest of the children, Rodrigo, Eduardo and Victor, for nine days we were in hunger strike and we received quite a lot of support. People in Chile knew that, because we made a phone call, we were in link with them, and the hunger strike was all over Europe, was a massive hunger strike, the dictatorship received quite a lot of pressure. They didn't give an answer, but in a way they recognised there was disappeared people.

M That was the first time they had to recognise.

V But they say that the people had fled the country, that they know they were about, and some of the people return and so on and they start to give evidence. Now all know that they are giving good information to us, that was very positive. And after that we continue to do this sort of cultural and political events. We were the people who founded the Nicaragua Solidarity Campaign before the triumph of the Nicaraguan regime.

When was that, Victor?

M It was '78, it was in our house. We join and we invited a woman, a British woman just arrived from Nicaragua and we met her by chance at the Tyneside Cinema, and she said, 'Oh, I'm just coming from Nicaragua, if you want some translation I would like to help you'.

What had she been doing in Nicaragua?

M   She was married to a Nicaraguan lawyer. She's living now in Chester-le-Street. She was quite a good supporter.

V   And in 1978 we launched the Nicaraguan Solidarity Campaign. Maria was in charge of the Nicaraguan Solidarity Campaign for quite a long time, five years.

M   A lot of time what we did was with other people not only by myself, first Patricia, then Claudia, then myself. We did a lot of day schools, we did a lot of sponsor work and we did demonstrations asking for support, and petitions, showing films, the Tyneside Cinema put the films on for us.

V   Also we help to launch the brigadista campaign to go to Nicaragua from Newcastle.

M   Yes, that was about '81.

When were you confident that the Sandinistas would win? From very early on?

M   Yes, because in our organisation we have a lot of discussion about that, and we say we have to learn a lot from the Nicaraguans, especially from the Sandinistas, they were teaching us a lesson, even that small country, was poor, and with the strength to go through and when they triumph, – it was on the television – you can't imagine how we felt here; it was magnificent. We went to the University, distributing leaflets and demonstrating outside the Union, it was wonderful. We having a lot publicity, just from a few leaflets, that was all, but we spent days and days asking for petitions. We did a lot of meetings, we invite people who had been in Nicaragua, there was a Nicaraguan student who have relatives, he just came, as representing the Nicaraguans, the views of Nicaraguans. And later we organise quite good events with the Third World First group especially, they were quite supportive. We organise stalls and food events for Nicaragua at the University and the Polytechnic.

Members of the Nicaraguan Solidarity Campaign with Maria and Victor and their daughter Raquel on the left.

When were you first involved with Nicaragua? When were you first aware of the effort?

M   Well it was 1977, '76. Well, we knew they were fighting, we knew that, but we making mistake, we were not really very confident at the beginning, well still we were troubled by what happened to us, it was a bad defeat that, we never thought at that time they were going to succeed, but in 1977, '78, we knew the advance of the Nicaraguans, the Sandinistas, and we start to regain confidence again, and start to support and talk about that.

And were you quite familiar with Nicaragua? Did you know what was happening? Did you know about Somoza?

M   We knew because we started to gather information and to ask.

V   Everybody knew, every Chilean who was involved in politics knows about Somoza. We read the newspaper in Chile, we knew about Somoza, we knew that he was a dictator. But here it was so difficult to find news about what happening in Nicaragua in 1977, for example, sometime the news that we receive was though our organisation who already got some Chileans in Nicaragua joining the Sandinistas fight. Some people who were in exile in England flew to Nicaragua and we were well informed about many things through the solidarities.

M   In 1980 one of the companeras living here in Newcastle, Patricia, went to Nicaragua, and that was very good because she brought information, she brought a pool of information, books, magazines, full of information, that was amazing and that allow us to do very very good thing indeed, and spread the good news.

After the Nicaraguan revolution did you spend more and more time working with the Nicaraguan Solidarity Campaign? Did that become more of a priority?

M   Yes it did, it was full time!

V   We did catering as well, sometime not very often, but anytime when somebody approach to us, we say 'yes'.

M   And everybody ask for empanadas.

V   Also I said we were one of the founders of the Salvadorean Solidarity Campaign. But Claudia put a lot of work and effort into that.

When was that? When did you start that?

M   It was in 1979 because we had the Latin American Society at the University and we start to invite some Salvadorean refugees already here in England and organise meetings and discussions. Claudia help a lot with the Salvadoreans, she did a lot, and Rodrigo, our son, he did more solidarity work as well. I decided to take a course in English at the college, which didn't allow me to do a lot of solidarity work. This was '81, it does not mean I stop to contribute.

In these years from when you arrived in Newcastle, was it very difficult to get work? Were you trying to find work to support yourselves as well?

V   I tried so many times. I went to the Job Centre many times but all the jobs that they offered were absolutely rubbish paid. We decide that our priority was to work in solidarity movement with our people, but also if we find a job here in England we have to work as an ordinary person, as every working class, English working class, do. I spent most of the time, I spent about five, maybe six, years working in an Indian restaurant washing dishes, and from there I start to save money to go back. When we decide to go back we take very seriously the saving but when I thinking back how much time I spend doing this bloody thing for so little money, but it was the only possibility. If they pay me less I was working anyway because I don't want to stay at home, it was mentally no good. I always work in Chile.

Could you tell us a little more about that.

V   I was in school till I was 18, because I was so lazy, I repeat it, twice. Then one year military service and I spent couple of year with nothing to do, just looking for job. I didn't know what to do with my life, I was so young, so immature, so absolutely lost in the world and really, really did not know what I wanted. And then I found a job, I worked for a while there and then I left, and then I found another job and then I left.

M   But first he found me!

V   And then I start to work as a DIY salesman in Santiago for many years and then I lost that job and I didn't want to go back to do the same job. At that time I had my professional licence to drive and then I started to work as a driver, as a minibus driver.

But you met Maria before you had the job?

V   I was married before with Maria.

M   We had two children when he joined the buses,

V   I was unemployed with two children,

M   was awful,

V   for maybe six months without any social security, nothing.

What did you do, Victor?

V   I met a man who used to work with me in the DIY business and he told me, 'Victor, I have a brother who work in the bus company as a inspector, go there and ask him to help you'. I went there, I talk to the man. 'If you are friend of my brother, you are my friend,' he said. 'I am going to help you'; and he call some other drivers and said, 'well, I need some help for this man, he's a driver, I know him very well', (he lie). The next day, he told me, come tomorrow. I knew the roads but I didn't know how to ride this minibus. I didn't know how to cut the ticket to give the passenger, and people give me the money and I don't know what to do, to receive with one hand or with other hand, and people looked at me wrong, but I made my first trip, it was very well, no problem at all; I felt more confident. The next day I had another trip with a different minibus, and on the fifth day I think, the man who gave me the first job say to me, 'you want to work for me full time?'. I say 'yes'. I

start to work full time, without paying any tax or nothing, it was the way in which the boss want you to avoid paying. And after that I have a contract. I work from 1960 to'67 sort of thing, and then I start to rent a better house for the family but I think we were living on a very very narrow wage. There were five children, Maria couldn't work and I had to supply all the money and it wasn't really enough. It was difficult, we had to dress five children, feed five children, was quite a lot.

And a dog, you had a dog?

M   Yes, Sultan.

V   But the dog was an easy thing to do, because he was a very humble dog, he would eat anything you put in front of his mouth, he never complained.

M   Raquel put her hand inside his mouth all the time and he didn't move, and Pedro also, they loved that dog.

V   He was beautiful, a mixture of alsatian and ordinary dog. He was stupid. Somebody gave him to me when he was just a little tiny thing, full of flea, and we cleaned him and start to give him meal, and my plan was always to train him to take care of the house because it was a lot of robbers in the area. He never did nothing and everybody can go freely inside the house, he never moved all day, he never barking, he was so stupid.

M   He wasn't stupid, we loved him.

What happened to him?

M   We left him.

V   Nobody wants a dog, because nobody want to feed a dog, people in the area had no money to feed their own children. Maria offer the dog to some friend and they said we like to have him but they couldn't afford to keep a dog, to feed a dog.

Oh, that's really sad.

M   Very sad.

Maybe we can talk a bit about how you got involved in the co-op.

V   I remember we met Nigel through Claudia. One day we were talking, we have a concert organisation problem, we have a concert and seeing we will be short of food and I went to Nigel's house and I said, 'will you come and provide with trays of pizza for us?'; I explain to you that we would be pleased if you can do cheap for us because it will be for a concert, for a benefit, and I explain to you, and you say yes. Later we met a couple of time and I ask again for another pizza. A year past and we were talking and one day you say if I was interested to do part time here in the restaurant and I came here one day to work when Melanie was working. I remember very clear that you didn't tell me that I have to work alone. I came here and Melanie was cooking and I say, 'well, here I am', and she say 'well Victor, there is this thing, that thing and that thing and you have to do this thing, okay?' and I say 'yes, thank you very much', and she said 'well I see you sometime'. I said 'excuse me, are you leaving me alone here?' and she say

'yes'; 'nobody's coming to work with me?' and she say, 'I don't think so'. So I had to do alone, cooking for people, but I was in here I was panicking, and I was furious, if I saw this man I ought to kill him. Luckily I have a very good day. It was a lot of customer, I don't know how I managed, I really don't know how I managed; I served everybody, I cleaned the tables, and I leave the kitchen clean and tidy, and also I make more money than people do during the week, I don't know how. I was really tired when I reach home, but I was very, very proud of myself, I say, 'Victor, you mananged'.
Thank you Victor.

M   You came to the bakery sometimes.

V   And work there as well. And then talking to you I remember you mention the idea to form a co-op. To be honest I didn't pay too much attention to this thing because I think it was one of the daft ideas that nobody could manage even during the war! But one day you mention to me if I would be interested to join the co-op and I say 'I don't think so'; it wasn't clear in my mind really at that time. But I went home and talking to Maria said, 'Nigel was talking to me to create a co-op' and Maria said, 'what did you say? Why don't you go say yes' and I say 'well, probably yes, but do you know how much implication will have for us?'. And Maria say 'I think it will be a wonderful thing'. I said, 'Maria, are you sure you want to work?' And she say yes. 'Okay' I said. And then I came to you, I said 'Maria and me are going to join the co-op'.
Before that hadn't you been involved with the Latin American days just after we opened for the very first time? When was that, Maria? When were you in Nicaragua?

M   1987, January to April.
The wholefood shop started in October 1985 and I supplied them with bread and stuff and in November next year, 1986, I started doing some work on the place and we actually opened the cafe just in the back in February '87, you must have started just after, when Maria got back from Nicaragua, as you say. And then in 1988, October 4th? we opened as a co-op.

V   Yes, it was very early October, because we just flew back from Spain the day before, and I came in the morning, very early in the morning, Maria came later, but I knew it was the day to open the co-op, and I came about 9.30 the opening day of the co-op.
So now, what about plans for now? Tell us a bit about what you will be doing when you go back to Chile?

M   Well the first thing is going to be mainly to adapt to our new country, because that is the reality, it's not the Chile we left. And that is going to take a while, but that is not going to stop us carrying through our dream to have a community project, and that is the priority, to start the project, to start our new life. There one of the main thing is to be feeding you with information and feeding you back with what we are doing and how is the life there, what is going on, because we know is a lot going on now. And also to slow down,

not just to speed very very quickly, that could be a mistake. That is really, and also we are going to have a little break, it's a good thing to do for start. *So will you try to find somewhere to live for the first few weeks? You won't have anywhere to live to start with.*

V   That will be the first priority, to try to find a place to live.

M   And at the same time to find what is going on, going places and going around.

And trying to find some old friends?

M   Yes. It's quite interesting, when Victor Ludwig was there he already contacted a few friends, and they know we are going back, they are waiting for news, and some of our friends are really prepared to work if that can, that is quite remarkable, a good thing, it is good to know that.

Have you a clear idea of what your community project will be Maria or are you waiting until you've lived there and work and see what is appropriate to the community? Are you clear that a women's skills workshop in woodwork will be a really significant thing?

M   I think it will be quite relevant to carry on with the project we have been organising here and to establish as a community project not as a business. It is going to be hard at the beginning, but we will see, we have the experience I think, to improve. But the important thing for us is in trying not to.be thinking in a profitable project just into provide some help; not to be Samaritans or something like that, just to involve people to do something and to pass a skill and to share in experience with them, that is one thing. Having written the project we know we are probably find difficulties to implement properly but we have to be patient, that is what I say, we have to adapt to the new Chile.

V   For my part I will, I'll work very closely with Maria to support the project as well. I knew a little bit of carpentry as well, I will give some help, I don't want to interfere too much because she absolutely capable to do the things, but if she need a help I will. For my part we are thinking with my son Victor about various alternatives to do something to live. One of these is the possibility to establish a workshop of motor mechanic repairs, it could be very very possible. If not probably we will try to establish a small shop to sell spare parts, which can be profitable as well. I would prefer the other one, I do not want to be a salesman, but then again something would have to be done because we have to live, we cannot depend on charity. What I have been thinking is to use the experience we have here in doing all the food and learning all the time how to provide good food and do it cheap not wasting any money. I am thinking I would like to help improve food for the children in the soup kitchens and places like that. I think that would be a good thing, to continue in some way what we have learned here.

Mote con Huesillos
Apricot dessert and drink

Chile
serves 6
Vegan

This dessert is very popular in Chile because it is healthy and nutritious, so children are often given this instead of fizzy drinks. When you ask the campesinos in the countryside for a cool drink of water they will usually offer you mote con huesillos.

250 g (9 oz) hunza apricots
175 g (6 oz) pearl barley
1 tbsp demerara sugar
½ cinnamon stick

Boil the cinnamon stick in 1¼l (2 pints) of water for 2 minutes, then add the hunza apricots and boil for 2 minutes more. Leave to soak overnight.

Early the next morning wash the barley and put to soak in 1¼ l (2 pints) cold water for about 3 hours. Then boil the barley in the water in which it has been soaking, for about 20 minutes. Check the water level and add more if needed as this reduces quickly. When the barley is very soft add sugar and allow to cool.

Mix with the apricots and put in a bowl in the coolest part of the fridge.

This can be strained and the liquid served as a cold drink and the apricots and barley served as a sweet by themselves or with other fruit and a topping of cream or yoghurt. Alternatively the whole lot can be stirred and served in big glasses with the apricots and barley distributed evenly among the liquid. It's delicious!

Atole
Maize drink

Nicaragua
serves 6

This is a good drink for breakfast, it has a very thick consistency. You could add different fruit flavours to make it more attractive. The first time I tried was in Nicaragua on a very hot day and Margarita, the old woman who made this drink, served it very hot. But later I drank it and I felt quite full and refreshed, and most of all very happy to meet Margarita who earns her living serving this lovely drink, every day for nearly 45 years.

50 g (2 oz) maize flour
1 l (1¾ pints) full cream milk
175 g (6 oz) demerara sugar
225 g (8 oz) fresh fruit pureed (e.g. melon, peach or guava) or chocolate
pinch nutmeg
pinch cinnamon

Dissolve the maize flour in 575 ml (1 pint) water. Heat the milk and when boiling pour in the maize flour. Do not stop stirring and boil for 3 minutes, then add sugar, nutmeg, most of the cinnamon and fruit puree.

Serve hot or cold in a deep bowl, sprinkled with cinnamon.

Arepas de Manjar con Sherry
Paper thin pancakes with caramel and sherry   serves 6

This is a mixture of recipes from several Latin American countries. Caramelized milk, manjar, is quite popular all over Chile. It is cheap to make a birthday cake and fill it with manjar.

2 eggs
175 g (6 oz) plain flour
275 ml (½ pint) milk
3 tbsp oil
3 tbsp sherry
340 g (12 oz) tin condensed milk
1 small pot, double cream, whipped

Make the batter by placing the flour in a bowl. Pour in the eggs and mix slowly, then pour in the milk, again mixing slowly to avoid lumps. Leave to stand a while.

Put the tin of condensed milk in boiling water and boil for 1½ hours until caramelized; this makes manjar. When cool pour ¾ of the tin into a small bowl and mix with sherry.

Make the pancakes in the traditional way, frying in very hot oil. It is very important to make them very thin. Leave to cool, then spread the manjar on each pancake and fold twice. Place 2 pancakes on each plate and cover one corner with cream.

Gatos Encerrados
Deep fried cheesy bananas

Ecuador
serves 4

225 g (8 oz) bananas
200 g (7 oz) cheddar or gouda cheese
1 egg
75 g (3 oz) white flour
150 ml (¼ pint) milk
2 tsp demerara sugar
½ tsp vanilla essence (or any essence you like)
275 ml (½ pint) oil for frying
treacle, maple syrup or honey to serve

Prepare a batter with milk, egg, sugar, flour and vanilla essence.

Cut bananas into 3, then slice lengthways, getting 12 slices from each banana [about 5mm (¼″) thick and 8 cm (3″) long]. Cut slices of cheese of a similar size. Place a slice of cheese between 2 slices of banana.

When you have all ready, heat the oil. Then cover the slices with the batter and deep fry them. Keep in a warm oven until ready to serve.

Serve with treacle, maple syrup or honey.

Torrejas de Arroz
Sweet rice fritters

Chile
serves 6

150 g (5 oz) white flour
100 g (4 oz) white rice
2 eggs, beaten
200 ml (7 fl oz) milk
2 tsp baking powder
50 g (2 oz) icing sugar
1 tsp cinnamon powder
pinch salt
oil for deep frying

Wash the rice and put to cook in plenty of water [about 1 l (2 pints)] with a pinch of salt. When cooked rinse with cold water and cool.

Sieve all the dry ingredients and then add eggs, milk and cinnamon. Mix thoroughly and add the rice; mix again.

In a deep frying pan heat the oil. When hot make fritters using a generous tbsp of rice mixture. Serve hot sprinkled with icing sugar.

GLOSSARY

BEANS/PULSES
Preparation: It is important that beans are prepared with care. First they should be picked over for sticks and stones and washed thoroughly to remove dirt. Lentils do not need soaking but larger beans should be soaked overnight in plenty of water. If you are short of time, boil for 3–5 minutes in a pan of water and leave to stand for 1 hour. The beans should then be drained, rinsed and brought to the boil in a pan of fresh water. Rapid boil for at least 10 minutes to remove toxins. These are present in raw beans, especially red kidney beans, but are made harmless by soaking and vigorous boiling. Next, turn down the heat and simmer the beans, partially covered, until tender. Cooking time varies according to the type of bean and the age of the crop. Drain the cooked beans and keep the cooking liquid for stock.

CHILLIES
These vary considerably from one variety to another. Generally red chillies are hotter than green ones and small chillies are hotter than larger ones. It is important to handle them carefully as their irritant properties may burn the skin. The chilli is hottest at its broader end where the seeds are concentrated. In order to impart the chilli flavour without too much of the hotness the seeds can be removed by cutting the top off the chilli and rolling it vigorously between the palms of the hands; the seeds should drop out easily from the cut end.

CORN MEAL (MAIZE MEAL)
This is made from ground, dried corn kernels and may be fine or coarse. Do not confuse with the highly refined white cornflour which is more familiar in western cookery.

FRESH CORIANDER
Usually, only the top leafy part of this aromatic green plant is used, in much the same way as parsley might be, for its flavour or as a garnish. It can be obtained from good Asian foodstores, or is easy to grow.

HERBS
Dried herbs may be used in place of fresh herbs but it is important to reduce the quantity by about half and to introduce them earlier in the cooking process. Fresh herbs should always be added at the last minute to retain their flavour fully.

OILS
A wide range of vegetable oils is available. Authentic Latin American cookery is heavily dependent upon corn oil which is ideal for stews, casseroles and for frying. Other light oils, such as sunflower or safflower make satisfactory substitutes.

ONIONS
In Chile onions are traditionally chopped very fine and fried in very hot oil. This imparts a unique flavour and texture to Latin American dishes.

PLANTAINS
These are large members of the banana family and can be used either green or ripe, in soups or as a vegetable. They must always be cooked are are never eaten raw. They are available from Asian and West Indian foodstores.

SWEETCORN
Several recipes ask for frozen sweetcorn. Fresh corn can be used but the frozen variety is easier to prepare and is picked while young and tender so it is likely to give a creamier result. Tinned corn is not recommended as it tends to be soggy and salty.

TORTILLAS
Originating from Mexico, tortillas are a kind of round, flat, unleavened bread with a wide variety of culinary uses.

Index

[V] indicates that the recipe is, or can easily be, Vegan.